LONGINGS AND LEGACIES:

IRISH PERSPECTIVES ON THE NEW MILLENNIUM

GW00671940

By the same author:

Issues, not Tissues

Bloom not Gloom

Mixed Messages

Be Your Own Friend

Longings and Legacies:

Irish Perspectives on the New Millennium

Ann Marie McMahon

ASHFIELD
Press

This book was typeset by KRISTIN JENSEN for

ASHFIELD PRESS
an imprint of
Blackhall Publishing
26 Eustace Street
Dublin 2
Ireland

e-mail: blackhall@tinet.ie

ISBN: 1 901658 19 8

A catalogue record for this book is available from the British Library.

Printed in Ireland by
Irish Lithoprint

CONTENTS

PART III: WRAPPING IT ALL UP

Acknowledgements

To Gerard O'Connor and his 'A' team at Blackhall Publishing – Tony, Claire, Eunice, Leonie and Kristin – you have done it again. Well done and thank you.

To my editor Kristin, who winged her way from the US to not only superbly edit but also typeset this book.

To Irish Lithoprint for their powerful printing.

To the Creative Inc. design team for their wonderful cover.

To Mary Claire for giving me a kick start to get the book up and running.

To Eileen, Orna and Patricia for assistance with typing and the computer.

To Rosario and Rosaleen for assisting with the questionnaires.

To John for his help with the proofreading.

To all the willing participants for their time and energy.

To An Taoiseach, Bertie Ahern, for your loyalty and support.

Thank you all so much and happy 21st century.

Dedication

Longings and Legacies is dedicated to Maria Falvey Purcell, who sadly passed away on 8 July 1999, leaving her husband, parents, brother, daughter aged eight and two sons, ten and twelve.

When Maria told me a year ago that she had cancer, I did not know what to say. Instead, I put on a Donna Summer tape, poured her a glass of wine and we danced as we did in the early 1980s to her music on the sun-kissed islands of Greece.

I shall always remember Maria for her sense of fun, adventure and vitality. She embraced life with enthusiasm, be it her fondness for history and politics at UCD where we studied together or her special love for children's books when she diligently worked as a librarian at Limerick County Library.

Maria had tremendous longings and desires for this world. She particularly wanted children to absorb books and learn from an early age. She had terrific plans to fulfil dreams to commence training courses for adults in this field and she wanted to start up an aftercare programme in Limerick for those suffering from cancer like herself.

She fought a brave battle for a whole year, with courage, dignity and an understanding of humans that she had not encountered until she was struck down with this terrible disease. Throughout the year she travelled weekly to attend her therapy sessions at Arc House, which she clearly enjoyed. She realised there were many worse off than she and she never complained. She was above self-pity and the 'poor me' trap.

Though out roads took huge diversions in our 30s, we came together for her final journey. Each week we met in a Dublin hotel after her therapy sessions where we ate and drank like two teenagers. She then went on to Trinity College to learn more about books. I marvelled at her enthusiasm. We had planned on having another fling in a far-off country to celebrate her recovery, but sadly, in early April the news was not good. However, we decided we would have instead an Irish holiday in Donegal or West Cork. We always looked at options. From Goa to Galway we shared many fantasies, longings and desires.

In late May, as we celebrated the final *Late Late Show* together in style at the Mater Private Hospital, Maria sang her heart out with Christy Moore, remembering times gone by. Whether it be singing, dancing, walking barefoot on the beach at Sandymount or Sutton or playing with Zeba, my new kitten, I was privileged to share that journey with her.

Maria, I may be here, but I know you are not far away, urging me on with that twinkle in your eye and your zest for life. Don't worry, we will have that toast at the launch.

Thank you,

AM

Foreword

When Ann Marie asked me to write the foreword to this book, I was very much struck by the title. In my own life I have been privileged to fulfil many of my own desires and am happy to be working in a position that can influence others on a daily basis.

However, I am also deeply aware of others who do not have the tools to fulfil their dreams and live in less than desirable circumstances. I hope my time in government will help those less well off to benefit in some way, and that I can leave a legacy of hope for those coming after.

I would like to congratulate Ann Marie on this, her fifth publication. I am delighted to be associated with this book that is celebrating our passage into the 21st century.

In 1993 she asked me to launch her first book, *Issues Not Tissues*, when I was Minister for Finance. I remember her saying to me, "Keep reading the books – one day you'll be Taoiseach." Little did I realise we would both fulfil our aspirations.

I hope the readers of this book will be able to realise their dreams and live a life in the 21st century that is both fulfiling and rewarding.

Bertie Ahern, *An Taoiseach*

Preface

In the beginning was the word...

It is through words that we send messages, be it verbally, via the media, or through the more recent and advanced form of communication, the Internet.

Words can convey different meanings depending on language, interpretation, culture and intonation. When we string words together, they can convey information and knowledge that can be handed down from one generation to the next. Words capture life at any given time, and through the power of language we have learnt about the lifestyles of those who lived during other eras.

At the dawn of the 20th century there was a great deal of optimism as people put the Victorian era to sleep and bade farewell to the famine. They looked forward with hope, aspirations and a feeling that there was light at the end of the tunnel.

The 20th century brought about an economic boom, the end of world wars, the first aeroplane flight, electric light, the telephone, television, computers and of course, for Ireland, the peace process. It was an era of creativity and progress, from the discovery of penicillin to man landing on the moon. We were moved by the sound of rock 'n roll, the words of modern poets and writers and by the images of artists and designers who have made Ireland *the* place to be in the approaching 21st century.

Yet who is steering us into the next millennium? Who will dominate throughout the 21st century and influence the up and coming generations? Is it the self, the family, the community, the politicians, the ecclesiastic experts, the business and financial leaders, the media moguls, the entertainers or academicians? Who exactly are these people, and what are their dreams and aspirations for the 21st century?

Longings and Legacies looks at the desires and resolutions of a variety of Irish people, from the words of children and teenagers to the voices of a sound-minded male and female who have touched their hundredth year. These people continuously shape and alter Irish society, and in this book they give us a hint of their desires and dreams that can be handed down to the next generation, who will carry the knowledge on and on.

Rubaiyat of Omar Khayyam
of Naishapur

I

AWAKE! For Morning in the Bowl of Night
Has flung the Stone that puts the Stars to Flight:
   And Lo! The Hunter of the East has caught
The Sultan's Turret in a Noose of Light.

II

Dreaming when Dawn's Left Hand was in the Sky
I heard a Voice within the Tavern cry,
   "Awake, my Little ones, and fill the Cup
"Before Life's Liquor in its Cup be dry."

III

And, as the Cock crew, those who stood before
The Tavern shouted – "Open then the Door!
   "You know how little while we have to stay,
"And, once departed, may return no more."

IV

Now the New Year reviving old Desires,
The thoughtful Soul to Solitude retires,
   Where the WHITE HAND OF MOSES on the Bough
Puts out, and Jesus from the Ground suspires.

Translated by Edward Fitzgerald

PART I:

PERSPECTIVES ON THE NEW MILLENNIUM

Chapter 1

THE PAST AND ITS PEOPLE

*"Ten, nine, eight, seven, six, five, four, three, two, one –
Happy New Year!"* When it is the year 2000, people
all around the world will be heralding in the new
century, from the jet-set rich who hop from one
country to another, to the drunkard who will probably be fast asleep, oblivious to the toll of bells,
chimes, or even pots and pans. Projections and post-
mortems will be held in the months leading up to
and immediately after the year 2000. We will all be
evaluating the effects this significant event will
have on all our lives. Some of us will use it as an
opportunity to reflect, contemplate and muse over
past misdemeanours and take pride in major
achievements. New decisions will be called for and
goals will be set with the gusto that comes from the
realisation that none of us will ever herald in a new
millennium again.

Such an event brings with it the usual remind-
ers of getting older, and perhaps even a yearning
to wind the clock back and start all over again. Of
course, this is one thing that can be shared by both
men and women, since we are all moving in the
same direction. While the modern emphasis might
be on retaining one's youthful image and somehow
trying to bypass the infamous mid-life crisis, at
some point there comes a realisation that we are
all on the same road, heading in the same direction
where the end result is the same.

Yet in between birth and death we are all living, and some far more happily than others. Outside influences certainly have a large part in determining our state of well being, and issues, such as culture, parenting, the environment, finance and health, all support the individual, allowing him or her to be the person he or she really wants to be.

If you are warmly welcomed into this world, your chances for happiness will be far greater. It is akin to putting a good foundation on a house – if the initial ground is shaky, you will have a lot of catching up to do and most likely will have more hurdles to jump over. Everyone strives to live an easy and stress-free life. Some of us might even spend our time daydreaming about a life without the daily hassles of finances and stormy relationships that interfere with our quest for happiness and ease. Some of us lead extremely complicated lives and always feel out of control.

"If only I wasn't...I would have a better life." "I should have...many years ago." "I must...and it will make it all OK." Self-doubt goes hand in hand with low self-esteem, and usually shatters any hopes of happiness and well being. Throughout the ages, there has always been a struggle for contentment, and while each decade brings new ideas and hope to a nation there is always a personal inner struggle for people to find their own values, principles and beliefs.

On a daily, weekly or yearly basis, individuals can experience enormous changes. Fate sometimes deals strange cards that lead us either on a direct road or one with endless twists and turns. Sometimes it may seem like an endless struggle, with no lights shining. At other times it may be confusing when trying to adapt to society's changes, be they domestic, professional or global transitions.

Throughout the last century, technological changes have occurred rapidly. In any decade we will always be trying to accommodate new ideas and communicative developments, so while technology might intimidate us, at the end of the day it is yet another tool to improve wider communication. The 20th century could be labelled the century of computers, and there is no doubt that technology has soared. Yet while we appear to be connected and 'hooked up', many people still lead very isolated and lonely lives.

While we are constantly searching for techniques to improve our communication systems, we must also consider what we are doing to improve happiness for ourselves. Some of us live in the hope that things will get better, only to realise that this is as good as it gets. Others constantly go from one crisis to another as anxiety, fear, stress, loss and inner pain seem to dominate their lives. Somehow they never find that light at the end of the tunnel. Others thrive on blaming the rest of the world for their own misfortunes, while some people never seem to learn from their past mistakes.

Promises are constantly made, especially on New Year's Eve, to change bad habits, but alas, human nature being what it is, old habits die hard. Very often we revert to sluggish coping techniques that weigh us down rather than help us move forward. Resolutions made at the end of any year are always made with the notion of creating and initiating a better lifestyle. Despite our yearning for the perfect formula for living, resolutions do not guarantee a pathway to happiness and, in fact, these endless lists may even go hand in hand with endless struggles.

Struggles in life are both relative and unique to each human being. Some experience and perceive suffering and struggles as the pathway to heightened spiritual living. Others fall apart and live in a constant helpless state, looking on in envy at those who appear to have it all. We all get our share of ups and downs, but it is how we cope that separates the struggling from the striving. In between are the survivors and the others waiting for better things to come.

As we plan our celebrations, be it a glitzy bash or a quiet reflection, the reality is that each century creates new beginnings, so we will all be leaving a legacy behind. If you don't like what the 20th century left, then this is your opportunity to leave something for those coming after you. Each of us can make an impact or influence others in some way.

For instance, your decision to stop smoking may influence friends and family, even though it started out as a pain in your chest that you were concerned about. Your decision to give yourself more free time may make you realise that overloading yourself achieves nothing. Your decision to become more involved with others may mean someone else may take a leaf out of your book. Your decision to travel may mean others will enjoy your company. Your decision to create a better life means you leave a good and happy legacy. Your desire and willingness to carry out methods and strategies for a more peaceful and happy world means that the next century and its people will be the better for your contribution to this world.

Chapter 2

RELEASE AND REVEAL

"Let's celebrate" will probably be the theme song for revellers over the next coming months. No doubt many will throw caution to the wind and enjoy all the momentum of the millennium. For some, any excuse is an opportunity to let their hair down, become less inhibited and relax. Some do this easily, while others do it with the accompaniment of alcohol and nicotine, which helps to ignite the flames of excitement and passion.

Of course, the regular revellers usually have money, health and plenty of invitations that keep them going. But what of the majority of us who will be trying in our own inimitable ways to celebrate an event which occurs only once in a thousand years?

- so Will you be the life of the party or will you just be looking on?
- so Will you be tripping the light fantastic with the shakers and movers or will you be a couch potato?
- so Will you be setting off for pastures new or will you be counting the cost of last year's holiday?
- so Will you be celebrating in the company of a spouse and family or will you be yearning for a long-lost lover?
- so Will you be surrounded by family and friends or will you be alone?

ဢ Will you be stress-free or caught up in a crisis
   that controls your life?
ဢ In short, will you be happy or will you be sad?

Any event can have different meanings and inter-
pretations for different people. There is no doubt
that we have various agendas going on at any given
time. Some are obvious, some hidden, some well
intentioned and some not, some dressed up, some
disguised, some real and some imagined. Whatever
the final agenda is, it is yours and yours alone. It is
your concern at any given time. While others might
try to trivialise your concerns, pour cold water on
them or fail to listen to them, you still remain consumed with the subject matter and will until you
choose to let go. While the subject might cause anxiety and stress and absorbs enormous energy out of
your lifestyle, it is not until you make a decision
about it and change your attitude that you can relax and enjoy other situations.

We all strive for happiness in this world, but the
routes and directions we take can be varied and
individualistic. For some the route is always
straightforward, with no twists, no turns and no
upheavals, as if life only deals them sweetness and
contentment. Challenges and goals are accepted
and worked through with little discomfort. Support
is never too far away and they will seek it out if it is
not there. Difficulties are easily overcome and
thinking is positive.

For others, however, life does not seem as fortunate and reality can be very painful. There is no
doubt that fate can deal some hard blows, even to
the point of being cruel. Often there are no easy

answers. It is almost as if these blows fall to test their stamina. "I can't take any more" can be the cry of those who are constantly trying to make ends meet, overcome grief or are battling with the odds.

Sometimes this all feels like a vicious circle or a boomerang. Everytime you sort out one problem, another comes straight back at you. Sometimes it feels like there is no way out. Words like 'burn-out' and 'stress' become all too familiar. At that point we need to stop, take time out and look at what we can do to make our own situation more manageable and worthwhile. Instead of scratching at the surface, we need to look more deeply and find a new prescription and perspective for a better way to live.

- ๛ We need to look at things that are really making us unhappy, stressed out, anxious or exhausted.
- ๛ We need to look at how we think about ourselves and those connected to us.
- ๛ We need to change our attitudes to situations best left in the past.
- ๛ We need to stop projecting into the future, which has not even occurred yet.

Happiness is now. Unhappiness ages you and real happiness revives you. Seek out tools that lift you from your misery. Remember there are always options, new routes and new maps. Maybe you need to remap your life and realise that perhaps you are living someone else's. Perhaps your parents had brilliant ambitions for you that you failed to achieve. Their constant words of encouragement keep ringing in your ear as you try to fulfil their dreams, all the while not knowing what your own dreams are. Maybe you are always trying to impress others by creating images that you think will improve your relationship with them, only to realise that they have other things on their mind.

Try as hard as possible to let go of old habits that have only weighed you down. To practise these new ways and habits requires patience, persistence and practice. Eliminate unsavoury ways that prevent you from celebrating your own life. Use positive energy to create momentum to help you to go on. Don't have expectations that are too high. It may be useful to write down anything that will limit you, and resolve to abandon those habits.

Use your imagination. Start up by visualising where you would like to be. Ask yourself simple questions like:

- What do I really want?
- How can I achieve this?
- Who can support me?
- Where can I get this support?
- What is blocking me?
- Who is blocking me?
- What helps me to be more creative?

Create the kind of life you would like to have. Perhaps you thought that you could never change, relax and have a better life. Now, at the dawn of a new millennium, you, too, can create a better life for yourself.

Get out of the rat race if it is getting you down. Downshift and look at the alternatives. Create more energy in your life and focus on your new life changes. Discover what is fresh, discover what your strengths are and discover what is precious to you. Value these in the same way you would value a treasured possession.

As you celebrate the arrival of this new millennium, put a priceless value on your life without the appendage of the negativity that will prevent you from obtaining the freedom and the ability to revel and enjoy what the world presents to you.

Chapter 3

CLOGGED AND CLOA

The word 'clogged' may conjure up images of someone cooped up in their bed with flu-like symptoms. They are cloaked in blankets, trying to nurture and nurse themselves back to full health. Fortunately, for most of us this only happens in the winter season when we are protecting ourselves from the harshness of the cold weather and all it brings. However, some feel clogged with painful emotions and cloak themselves from society in order to survive as best they can. For some, life is a long battle with emotional pain, and without support the battle is always uphill.

Warning signs are often ignored when things go wrong, and some cope by lashing out, exhibiting their anger and aggression in a way that releases their inner distress at the expense of others. They may be unaware of their motivation for lashing out, but it is their way of coping when clogged with distressful emotions that they don't like. When something makes us feel uncomfortable, we move away from that discomfort. We do something to change the feeling of discomfort because we are motivated towards pleasure and a better way of life. Any sort of pain and discomfort from an early age is usually soothed away, and we automatically switch to comfort zones for relief from the pain. Humans share this technique with animals as we push away life's hurts and find strength and comfort in our support systems.

Positive people are generally goal-motivated and work towards achievement and getting results. They move in one direction and team up with like-minded people. Should they see an advertisement looking for a dynamic, self-motivated individual, they would not hesitate to answer the advertisement, because they see themselves as the type of person the ad requires. However, people clogged with emotional baggage would move away from answering it because they feel that they are not good enough, deserving enough or capable of what the ad requires. These individuals are usually pessimistic and consumed with problems, often digging up the past and projecting fear into the future. Happiness is short-lived because it is not familiar enough to them to believe it will last.

How we are motivated is often tied up with our value system. Those who are goal-oriented usually achieve their end and are more socially accepted and valued. No doubt it is easier for them to cope if they are constantly rewarded, and in the long run the effort becomes both effortless and second nature to them. Some people are goal-driven in a naïve fashion. They fail to consider problems and difficulties that may set them back temporarily. They may have to learn the hard way and may have to overcome many side kicks and knocks before they learn the art of not putting their foot in it.

To be unmotivated is not a pleasant feeling. People lacking in purpose or direction are often low in energy, have little confidence and find life an uphill battle. Some constantly examine why they are like this and try to evaluate the reasons for it. Others turn to all sorts of props to get the engine oiled. Drugs, alcohol and even nicotine become lifelong habits when healthy coping techniques have failed. However, drugs of any kind are only a temporary support and usually end up creating secondary problems. Giving them up is a problem in itself and is often a difficult task. In fact, what happens is that the particular drug becomes the motivating factor, and reality is thrown out the window. Sadly, the end result can be severe illness, dependency and finally death.

While professionals spend a lot of time trying to demotivate people from abusing substances, helping them to build self-esteem and self-confidence takes a back seat. Difficulties often multiply and complacency is perpetrated by the illusion that the drug is doing its job. Dependency becomes a way of life and realising that you can live without certain props becomes more and more difficult.

For somebody who may have been going through a period of demotivation, e.g. loss of a relationship or bereavement, how this period is handled will often determine how they will cope in other situations that might come their way. We all experience setbacks at different times of our lives. Sometimes it is a matter of literally sitting back and exploring what exactly is going on before making any rash decisions. Talking through problems can usually point individuals in the right direction. They will learn from mistakes or wrongdoings and will be able to move on with support and confidence.

However, demotivated people fail to accept that things will ever be right again and end up on a merry-go-round of hopping from one problem to another. Somehow they just cannot seem to get started on the right foot. Other physical symptoms may kick into action, such as insomnia, lack of appetite or overeating. In other words, the body doesn't like connecting with this negative mind because it is clogged and cloaked with emotional pain and turmoil. At times it might seem like there is light when someone offers a helping hand, but unless you work at ridding yourself of bad habits, be it in your mind or behaviour, you will fall back on old ways and return to where you started, trapped in your own misery.

Certain choices, methods and decisions need to be made if you want to go from being unmotivated to having good self-esteem and a positive outlook. Certain questions need to be answered and certain steps will have to be taken to make changes that will bring you happiness and contentment. Certain structures will have to be created to lay a foundation for stability and balance.

Change for anyone can be quite daunting, but if you start out making small changes that are attainable, you will realise that you can actually do it. We must also remember that we all have choices, but we have to learn how to make decisions and deal with the consequences that go with them. There are always options if the consequences are not to your liking; situations do not have to be black and white. As with any choice, you can exercise flexibility and aim for compromise. As long as one part of you starts to feel energised and motivated, you can spread this to other situations in your life.

Whether you are clogged with pessimism that

brings negative feelings and uncomfortable behaviour or are constantly cloaking yourself from others' criticisms, verbal attacks or judgements, remember that it is your perception and interpretation of this that causes the most upheaval. Whether it is rejection, denials, refusals or short-changing, remember that whatever feelings you have, they are yours, and the sooner you recognise or make friends with them, the better.

Learning to move from pessimism to optimism and giving yourself more hopeful experiences means eliminating past unhealthy behaviours, examining the present and exploring the future. Your recovery from unmotivation is about your discovery of motivation, and whatever helps you in your recovery should be permanently taken on board. You should set limits and create boundaries so that if you fall, your land will be softened. Rid yourself of anything that will bring you back on the road that disempowers you, and concentrate instead on what empowers you.

While we need to shelter ourselves from harsh environments, we can in turn enjoy spring and summer when they arrive. Nature knows how to look after itself and is always ready for different climates. In the same way, we have to learn to prepare ourselves for the social environment that has been constantly changing since time began. We need to plant the seed of optimism and be ready to watch it grow and blossom. Sometimes we need to just go with life, and if we are feeling positive we can take this in our stride. Like a good garden, we have to reap and sow, but also take out the weeds and replace the seeds as seasons dictate. Tuning in to nature and how it evolves is one way to look at creation in all its glory and realise that, on the grand scale of things, we are only one small part of the bigger picture.

Now is the time to leave those inhibitions behind, given that there is no better time than a new millennium to wipe the slate clean.

Chapter 4

QUAKE OR QUIVER

Did you ever quake in your boots over something you were dreading, or quiver and shake at the thought of something that will actually never happen? Either way, the underlying emotion is fear. Fear can grip your life to such an extent that you believe you cannot handle certain situations. When this happens, your state of mind changes and creates inner tension that seizes your body and prevents you from doing very ordinary things. Fear creeps up on you like a thief in the dark and steals away emotional well being. Some fearful situations include:

ഇ The thought of standing up in public.
ഇ The thought of taking an exam.
ഇ The thought of living alone.
ഇ The thought of getting older.
ഇ The thought of doing a driving exam.
ഇ The thought of failing.
ഇ The thought of making decisions just for everything to turn out wrong.
ഇ The thought of life not turning out the way you want.

In other words, we usually dread something that has not even happened yet.

The worst fear is of fear itself. Fear of the unknown comes from negative thoughts that allow you to project into the future and lets you believe your world will collapse. This is merely a state of mind, but it is so gripping that it will prevent you from dealing with daily situations. Fear has such a strong hold on you that situations actually become painful.

The longer you give in to fear, the harder it will be to move away from it. Some people handle their fear by becoming meticulous and perfectionist in manner, but this is only an attempt to control a situation, not solve it. Others inherit fear from another generation. In the past, people suffered from debilitating attacks of fear, but simply learned to live with it and felt that they were sent by God. These attacks manifested themselves in shyness, lack of confidence and isolating behaviour. Suffering from fear is like standing in a field with a tornado coming straight at you. Alternatively, it is as if a door shuts off the world and you don't hear anything except your own breathing and heartbeat. Fear can leave you threatened, vulnerable and unable to overcome life's many hurdles. Today, people can be helped through theraputic intervention and need not suffer in silence, in pain or in vain.

Fear affects us so strongly that we lose sight of other issues going on around us. Some fears are natural and can warn and protect us from dangerous situations. For example, smoke triggers fear, which in turn may prevent us being badly burned. When there is no clear signal and our feelings overwhelm us, the root cause may be in a situation that we never properly dealt with, which has now left us behaving in passive ways due to abandonment, rejection or even shame.

Some fears can relate to our perception of society and how others perceive us. People who feel like they're outside of society may fear rejection and end up rejecting themselves rather than realising that others are in the same position. This is a fear of being labelled, and can be exacerbated by a fear of being exposed and others discovering the so-called hidden skeletons in your closet.

Sometimes we cannot articulate what is going on, but we know we are not the same as others and that we are not going to be accepted by them. Not only do we fear the unknown and the future, we also fear being found out about who we are, afraid that somebody might see through us and note the discomfort we feel. Guilt plays a huge part in this, and while it may be of little use, it holds us back and endorses fear.

Some fears are so compounded that they become a full-time preoccupation. For instance, somebody with a social fear or phobia avoids encounters or meeting people because they feel inadequate. Life for them becomes a series of avoiding situations where they feel as if they are on show.

While certain anxieties start out as a response to stressful situations, unless they are dealt with they can lead to other problems, such as low self-esteem and low self-confidence. In some cases, you may end up turning to substances such as drugs or alcohol to ignore these issues.

You may avoid situations because you believe that it will stir up anxiety, and the longer this goes on, the worse it gets. Basically, you end up anticipating situations and expecting the worst, dwelling on symptoms that may or may not occur and fearing the symptom itself. This is the same for people who worry a lot – they end up worrying more about the problem than the solution. However, once you realise what is happening and realise the havoc it is causing in your life, you can decide to do something about it.

Initially you may need to get help, even professional help, in order to get started. Learning how to relax will help you in any situation. Learning how to cope in a small situation will help you when you have to deal with big situations. For instance, someone who has a fear of speaking in public could start off by giving a small talk in front of two people and then slowly move up the number until they can talk in front of two thousand people. You have to practise overcoming fear and do this regularly until the effort becomes effortless.

It is also important to acknowledge when you have overcome a fear and reward yourself. This builds self-esteem and confidence, and ultimately is about you managing your life in a more relaxed and fear-free environment. You will be surprised at your own accomplishments as fear disappears.

- හ You will learn to tackle situations with new energy and will be less threatened by others.
- හ You will discover how to meet your needs.
- හ You will connect with others and communicate with greater ease.
- හ You will discover that thoughts and images are no longer blurred.
- හ Energy will come back where it had been zapped before. In previously fearful and anxious situations you will notice the return of spontaneity,

self-assurance, respect and confidence for yourself.

ഇ You will be able to reach out to others and widen your boundaries.

ഇ You will tune in and become more aware of others' difficulties.

ഇ You will learn that there is an answer to any problem because you found the answer to yours.

ഇ Life will take on a new meaning and you will start to relax and enjoy it.

Sometimes, however, we can hear a voice in our heads saying, "It's alright for you" or "It's alright to know the answers, but how do you put the information into practice?" Sometimes we can exhaust ourselves reading all the books on the subject, but remain unable to apply all the advice they are giving.

How do you go about this? Start by selecting a time when you are going to talk to someone about your situation or write out a plan for yourself. Select small, achievable goals for overcoming your fear. Visualise yourself being more confident and in charge. Remember: you are on the road to overcoming your fear. If it is still daunting after reading this, talk it through with friends and keep in mind that your intention is positive and achievable.

Let's look at a hypothetical situation where your fear may paralyse you. You have been invited to a dinner party related to your work, but you feel totally socially inept. Your fear is about the ability to communicate confidently in a social situation. You feel that everyone is better than you are and that they lead more interesting lives than you do.

In this case, you should focus on your own interests and abilities and try not to run yourself down by building others up in your own head. Invite some of your friends over for a trial dinner to give yourself a chance to practise being relaxed in others' company. Take note of what makes you feel at ease and build up your confidence in ways that suit you. Be comfortable with your appearance and your environment. Keep an eye on your goals and also on what energises you towards achieving these goals. Keep reminding yourself that you are in the process of achieving something and that if you make mistakes, it is okay. It is all a learning processes. At the end of the evening, evaluate all the positives and negatives and be prepared to congratulate yourself for your achievements. This is the first step to overcoming your fear in a social situation.

Even as we approach the 21st century, some will be clogged with the fear that planes will crash, computer systems will shut down and we will all be doomed. Some even go so far as to believe the world will end and plan for this by building their own bunkers. Earlier this year we had predictions from Nostradamus that the world would end in July 1999, and we're still here! Thus, the energy spent on worrying about this was pointless and useless.

The same could be said about any fear. As the cliché goes, the only real fear is fear itself. That is why it is so important to learn to live one day at a time and enjoy the present, for we have little control over the future. Let's leave a legacy of happy memories and happy events behind instead of our energy-draining fears.

Chapter 5

MOVEMENT AND MOTION

While we bade farewell to the 19th century, the 20th century became the century of movement. From the jazz age to rock n' roll to disco inferno, the 20th century brought people to their feet. All across the world, dance and movement came alive, and with the added luxury of television we were able not only to see the likes of dancers such as Fred Astaire and Ginger Rogers, we were also able to further enhance our dance repertoire and participate in all the dancing trends by watching music videos.

Each decade brings new trends, and those who latch on to fashions and fads are usually the adolescents whose bodies and souls come alive during puberty. There is no doubt that the time in life between being eleven and twenty-one is a very turbulent one. Boys and girls alike are going through hormone havoc with the transition from adolescence to adulthood. In fact, in addition to being the century of computers, the 20th century could also be dubbed the century of the teenager. Businesses all over the world have made fortunes from courting sixteen, seventeen and eighteen year olds, and have recently focused on children as young as eleven and twelve.

It seems that slick business people have put labels on everything. From designer clothes, perfumes, accessories and sports wear to gourmet foods, we are all being bombarded by labels. Teenagers are the most vulnerable to this, since they latch on to the seductive powers of advertising. Since it's trendy for teens to be one of the gang, marketing people are having a field day.

Women in the Western world have made incredible progress in the 20th century. No longer are they out of sight and silent. No longer are they veiled and cloaked. No longer are they a disgrace if they 'step out of line'. No longer do they have to stay at home and 'mind the house'. No longer have they a dirth of choices.

However, we must also remember that cultural values that are different than our Western ones still dominate women around the world. While the Western woman has been unveiled and given freedom to equal their male counterparts, in many countries many more women are still forced to obey laws that keep them oppressed. In these countries, women are not only poor but oppressed by men who see no reason to give women equality and a better life.

In the 21st century we should strive to eliminate such oppression. No person has the right to decide that one gender should be treated in a certain way. We are all human. Sometimes we are all weak or vulnerable and sometimes we all show incredible reserves of strength, and gender has nothing to do with this.

While in many cases men still control the purse strings of the world's economy, they can no longer continue their solo acts because women are constantly coming on board to shake, rattle and roll. The ideal world is like the perfect military two-step, with men and women gliding across the dance floor of life together, keeping their steps in harmony, swaying to the music, each hoping the other will keep their rhythm. Of course, when the music stops so does the dance. Like any ballroom dancer you can continue, give up, improve you rhythm, seek a new partner or try something new. In fact, we are all like ballroom dancers on the floor of life – if we do not practice, we will soon lose our skills and fail to tune into the rhythm and harmony that is all around us.

During the decade from our twenties to our thirties, we believe that the world is our oyster and we can glide and jive to whatever comes our way. We tend to try out anything in our twenties because we know that time is on our side. We can even postpone events to savour the fun of experiencing different lifestyles. It is almost like having a provisional licence and the loan of a car so that the full brunt of responsibility does not come our way. The thirties can be a time of either stabilising what you set down in your twenties or it can be a time to still set sights on new pastures. Of course, any age presents new crises and new opportunities.

Today the trend is to celebrate 'the big 40'. Some herald it in with the party to beat all parties, celebrating the fact that they have lived this long and no longer fear the future. Others do not see the need to put a stamp on any particular birthday and face getting older with a silent, inner contentment. This is something that they may practise every day, and they realise that time is passing and they are ageing on an hourly basis.

In the century gone by, people died younger due to ill health and lack of research in finding the causes of certain diseases. Today our life expectancy keeps growing longer. People in their fifties and sixties today have a surge of optimism that would have been unheard of so many years ago. It's like getting a new lease on life. Our thirties and forties, therefore, are merely trials for this second stage. More people are prepared to take risks that would have been out of their reach in years gone by. Others throw caution to the wind and decide that they now have the time and the money to really enjoy themselves. Others make up for lost time and with new-found wisdom they are getting ready for their eighties and nineties. Provided that you have both physical and mental health, you will be able to achieve your dreams, no matter what your age.

From our sixties on we still look at the path ahead but there is one issue that can not be avoided – death. We are all moving towards death, although many of us deny it because we are frightened by it. Heading towards our last dance, we should move with rhythm and harmony.

With death, the light at the end of the tunnel has gone out in somebody's life, but very often that life can continue to shine through in memories of them and the stamp which they have left on their loved ones or society. While death is defined as "The Last Dance", like any other great dancer we will always remember the deceased's rhythm, movements, music and their joy. Through their memory and our awareness of their lives we are reminded to live in the present and to value the human experience on the dance floor.

Chapter 6

SHADE AND SHADOWS

Did you ever find yourself sitting in the shade on a sunny day, aware that the sun was just too hot? Try as you might to get that golden tan while enjoying the summer season and sunlight, you have to acknowledge that occasionally something can get the better of you. You realise that if you expose yourself to the sun anymore not only will you scorch your skin, but you could end up with a deadly disease.

In the shade, you usually feel protected and you give yourself time to contemplate what you could or should have done. For instance, you may not have been wearing protection for you skin, and your age is also a factor. You evaluate what is going on and you make a decision about what to do. You choose to do something different, and therefore your time in the shade proved valuable. From now on you will find alternative ways of relaxing during the summer months.

Armed with this simple discovery, you realise that perhaps you can apply this formula to different areas of your life. Maybe you realised that the time-out in the shade gave you the chance to get a better perspective on other issues in your life and now you can see what is needed to protect you from getting scorched in other situations. We are all the sum total of our own decisions and experiences, but sometimes we are willing to go to extremes to achieve an end, and with a huge price to pay. Extremes in any aspect of our lives usually come at the expense of something else. We are better off finding a balance.

Some of us don't like the sun, since we never shine ourselves and always live in others' shadow. That could come from a lack of confidence or self-esteem to believe that we are really worthwhile. While culture, tradition and family values influence us in our early years, as we get older we usually break free and create our own agenda. However, some people always feel like they are living in the shade and shadow of others. Some are quite content to be there, and accept their role in the backseat while others drive forward. They do not want the limelight and all that goes with it, since they have not yet learnt how to control their own turbulent, topsy-turvy lives. They just feel that they never get things right, and even when they do, they are still not satisfied. They are constantly moving the goal posts, and this can all lead to huge discrepancies, particularly in relationships.

Relationships can make or break anyone. While we are born alone and die alone, in between we spend our time connected to some or trying to disconnect from others. Those trying to connect believe that those already connected have it made, and vice-versa. Getting it right can be a lifelong goal, but at some point we have to accept that no one has it all and that we are all struggling as best we can to do better.

Relationships are a major source of pleasure, but also of pain. Some of us have the resources to handle relationships and all their complexities, while others constantly search for what the best methods of coping are. This can be laborious, but it can also help us to find enormous inner strength.

Problems in relationships should be seen as a breakthrough rather than a breakdown. Anyone can improve their relationship skills if they are willing to take the time to learn, and by so doing can improve the quality of their lives. They may even learn to change how they view the world and will be more willing to explore different avenues. The art of relating to others well is a lifelong task, since we never know who is going to cross our path from day to day. If we are prepared for the unexpected we will cope admirably in any situation, but if we are always concerned with inner baggage we will get caught up in other issues.

We all have to take personal responsibility for where we are at in life and understand that none of us are perfect. There is personal freedom in choosing where you want to be and knowing that it is the right place for you to be. Always wishing life away only leads to unhappiness and inner turmoil. Constantly berating yourself for not being perfect only leads to further stress and strain. At some point we have to admit that we are doing our best, and that if we were capable of doing better, then we would be.

Some of us are always ready to jump in and sort others' problems out for them, particularly if we feel we have all the answers. We jump in when we hear familiar words or statements that seem applicable to our own past experiences. We often don't hear the full story and can go so far as to act as the judge, jury and prosecution. We can all be experts at sorting out others' problems and relationships, but very often we fail to empathise with what is really going on.

Sadly, people often have their own agendas that have nothing to do with the problems they are trying to solve. They have their own emotional baggage that blinds them, and misguided opinions often come into play. This can have devastating effects, particularly if the other person is vulnerable, impressionable and lacking in confidence.

When we play the role of expert with a friend who is going through a problematic intimate relationship, we should remember that there are always two sides to every story. Generally we only hear one side, and that one side can be twisted and tainted to suit our appetite for hot gossip.

We paint a picture that we want people to listen and respond to. We often have our own agenda and want particular answers. Sometimes we retell our story until someone comes up with the response we really want, whether it is right or wrong. Sound or unsound, we try to do out best at the time and we convince ourselves that others don't understand, don't care or interfere too much in our lives.

No matter what, we are all struggling and coping in the same world. Some of us may appear to get it right, but then again we may just be putting on masks or a good show to keep up appearances. Social etiquette may be more important than emotional happiness.

Some of us scoff at 'keeping up appearances'. Others are so enthralled with the show that they cannot distinguish between what is important and what is trivial. They may even pay a very high price just to keep up with the Joneses of the world. They get caught up in the whirlwind of society and the self gets lost in the shuffle.

There is no doubt that at different times of our lives we could find ourselves living in different situations. While some do not like living in the shades or shadows, they will all eventually learn to live in their own right and delight in their own efforts. As we approach the millennium, some of us will thrive in the limelight, supported by family and friends, or hide behind closed doors in the shadows of the party-goers.

Of course, there are those who will think it is all a bit over the top and refuse to change their usual New Year's habits, and perhaps will sleep and dream straight through the dawning of the millennium. Some may even use this time to make a fast buck and cash in on overpaid babysitters, waiters and waitresses, taxi drivers or those throwing the millennium parties.

Whether you dance away the night or sleep soundly through it, wandering through your own wonderful dreams, be at peace this New Year's Eve and enjoy.

Chapter 7

CELEBRATING THE CENTURY

"'Tis the season to be jolly, tra la la la la..." Christmas 1999 could be the supporting act that will warm us up before the onslaught of millennium fever. From bonfires to fireworks, we will all be part of one huge celebration as we explode into the new century. We will be acutely aware of which time zone we are in and aware, too, of the fact that we will not be around to see the dawning of the 22nd century.

We will look back in awe at the heroes and heroines of the 20th century who helped create the world we live in today, realising that we owe our health, comfort, economic boom and new lifestyle to these people. We have a thriving economy (our Celtic tiger), our peace process and our social partnership. We'll realise the 20th century started strong and ended even stronger.

We can tune in and connect instantly to people all over the world as a result of major advances in technology. Television has undoubtedly kept us all in touch, yet there is a mixed bag of messages in the images broadcast in homes all over the world, leaving us confused, searching for more answers and wondering what we are meant to think of what we are seeing. Some delight in being part of this new world, feeling that things can only get better. These people, though, may be unaware of the fact that, despite the enormous strides we've made in the last one hundred years, we still have a long way to go. Human suffering still exists, despite the enormous wealth enjoyed by some.

Many are overwhelmed as they realise how little they can do but look after themselves and their own small patch of the world. Others are determined to make the world a better place. Still others feel better living in the here and now before getting too old, too tired, or waiting until it's just too late.

While cultural influence will always dominate, we realise the world is changing. Ireland is now connected to Europe in ways unheard of one hundred years ago. Did we ever think Europe's finances would all be one? Did we ever dream we could fly across the world in a matter of hours? Did we ever dream we could connect with each other in mere seconds? The world is indeed getting smaller, and as we connect more closely we realise we are truly all the same. We are all on earth for a limited amount of time, and basically we all want to be happy. We want to feel good about ourselves and what we are doing.

Yet where we were born and what was available to us in our first ten years of life will determine the rest of our lives in significant ways. All children require nurturing and nourishment to feel that they belong in the world. Given the right circumstances, any child could thrive in any culture and adapt to its mores and customs quite easily. Children can adapt to any environment, providing it is welcoming and safe. It is only as they grow into adults that they have to navigate around and deal with negative influences or past deprivations that often come back in strange guises and unforeseen circumstances.

The 20th century certainly unearthed a lot of hidden cruelties that children suffered. The revelation that child sex abuse was amongst us and that we failed to see it should make us more aware in the next century for any signs of discontent among children. Where many of us once felt safe knowing that politicians and the Church were safeguarding our interests, we now know that they, too, have their own problems. We no longer believe that those who lead us are free from doing no wrong. On the other hand, we must not paint everyone with the same brush. The 21st century should be one of enlightenment and a chance to allow every person, regardless of age, creed, colour, gender or culture, to be free to pursue whatever positive opportunity that comes their way.

There should be a policy in place to include those impoverished not only economically, but also lacking in happiness and health, be it mental, physical or emotional. Without any of these, life can be a constant uphill struggle, and sometimes it feels as if doors just never open. Some, however, never experience this feeling of strife, since support systems seem to always be at their side. Perhaps they have learned early on that others constantly endorse their belief in themselves, and therefore life is comfortable.

Sadly, others seem to always experience hardship, and feel there is no end in sight. Some of these people wish the end would come sooner rather than later, and some have even brought about their own end because they saw no other way out. Those left behind may wonder where they went wrong.

Sometimes there just aren't any answers, and sometimes someone's death makes us realise something *can* be done. Maybe it was we who failed to listen or hear what was really being said to us. At any stage, life can take strange twists and turns. Some of us are ready for them, and some of us are not. However, we must all realise that there is always hope as long as we have the longing and desire for something better.

We should never write someone off for not being good enough, pretty enough, clever enough, capable enough or young enough. We all deserve a chance, and which of us can decide who deserves any more or less? *Longings and Legacies* allows us to peep in at people from all ages and walks of life, learning what their dreams and aspirations are for the 21st century.

It is interesting that those heading towards final retreat still have strong desires to achieve certain goals. So someone who wants to be a better artist still has vision and energy to achieve this. Even the 99-year-old yearns for a better life. While twenty somethings have wishes and yearnings to do things, this is also coupled with impatience and trepidations. No decade of 'somethings' feel they are not young enough, fit enough or wise enough to hope and long for a better world. The older generation has wisdom and while they perceive their bodies ageing they still have boundless energy. There is no doubt that while youth is wasted on the young, insight arrives with age as the ups and downs of life are handled and meaning is discovered. Young people are always in a hurry to prove to the world that they have made it but in fact no one ever really makes it.

Every day we experience the self in a world surrounded by contrasting perceptions of success and
failure, beauty and ugliness, haves and have-nots,
sick and well, living and dying, housed and homeless, heroes and victims, old and young, positive
and negative, conservative and liberal. From age
nine to ninety-nine, we are enmeshed in this world
of trends, generational gaps, gender issues and
mind-boggling images. Our perception of life is
always changing and will continue to change as
long as we are exploring new ideas. Science and
technology are stretching the human frontier, re-
producing, redesigning and even cloning nature.

At times we think we have it made or have it all
and wonder how we got this far. The reality is that
no one has it all, no one has totally made it and no
one is indispensable. Our perceptions and inter-
pretations of situations will always be individualistic. We are all only here for a short time, and are
preparing the world for the next generation. Our
investments in whichever field we choose to get
involved in may not show dividends in this life,
but people coming after us could reap from writers, artists, sports personalities, politicians, church
leaders, medics, media moguls, business people,
academics, parents, teachers, children, shop keep-
ers, journalists, helpers and entertainers of today.
We all are doing our best and most of us realise
this. Nothing should ever be deemed wasted or
regretted. By the dawn of the 22nd century we will
all have made a mark in this world. No one knows
what is around the corner. No one knows what it is
really like in the next world. But hopefully we will

all meet up and celebrate and enjoy each other's company. Happy 21st century and enjoy the new millennium.

PART II:

WORDS AND WISDOM OF THE IRISH PEOPLE AT THE DAWN OF A NEW MILLENNIUM

PREFACE TO
QUESTIONS AND ANSWERS

When I first came up with the idea for this book, I wanted to do something different. I wanted a book to celebrate the closure of the millennium and the commencement of another. I particularly wanted to involve others, if only to realise that my own thoughts are limited. I would like people in the next century to be able to remember and look back at how we Irish felt and thought at a particular time in history. Having explored other reading material I failed to discover how people really felt at the close of this century.

The only way I could achieve this was to literally ask people to give me their views. I set out two years ago on this journey by devising a questionnaire and mailing it to all types of people. The response was nine negatives to every one positive, which is an average response for any questionnaire. While I received many replies that said "thanks, but no thanks", many politicians were kind enough to reply, especially our Taoiseach, Bertie Ahern. Teenagers and those in their early twenties were receptive to the idea, while those in their thirties, forties and fifties sometimes had to contemplate and look into their inner selves to find their thoughts on the dawning of a new millennium.

There were times when I despaired, when the lack of responses found me thinking it was not such a good idea after all, but just one good response would encourage me all over again. I particularly enjoyed my early morning breakfast with Sr Stanislaus Kennedy, who not only responded, but involved all her co-workers and those who benefited from her work.

I made some telephone calls and sent some faxes. Replies came more quickly and I had the pleasure to talk to such people as Austin Currie, Tony Gregory and Sonny Knowles, to name just a few. Some were extremely unselfish and responded to the task with energy and enthusiasm. Some needed gentle prodding and persuasion. Some said an enthusiastic yes and then got cold feet and ducked out. Some froze at the word 'personal', particularly men. Some objected on the grounds that it was a commercial venture and some could not afford the time. Others just blankly refused and some never got around to replying due to busy schedules or simple forgetfulness.

Both the old and the young responded with vigour – the old had the time, the young had the zest. Whatever the response, I was enormously grateful to those who shared their dreams and were happy to leave a legacy behind. I extend a special thank you to Mary Manton, who participated through her own mobile computer. Mary cannot speak or walk, but her spirit and enthusiasm are enourmous. She certainly helped to make this book more inclusive.

The whole process made me realise that we are all just passing through this world on a journey. For some the journey is short, inspiring or fruitful while for others it is hard work, boring and endless. In our formative years we have the most spontaneity and enthusiasm, and at the other end as we approach old age we appear to have time. In between we are caught up in society's whirlpool of personal, domestic, social and career issues that can leave us energised and exuberant, exhausted or drained.

As it turned out I received sufficient replies to create *Longings and Legacies*. At the same time I enjoyed the journey in meeting such a wide variety of people, from our Taoiseach to Travellers, from the traders in Moore Street to elderly people in nursing homes, and from delightful, enthusiastic children to those helping and shaping our community.

A huge thank you goes out to each and every participant – you have helped shape this book.

(Editor's note: All answers have been reproduced as close to the original as possible.)

QUESTIONS

1. What will your resolution be for the millennium?

2. Which personal traits would you like to give up?

3. What are your dreams and aspirations, personally and globally, for the millennium?

Chapter 8

MAYOR'S MESSAGE

Councillor David Alderdice,
Lord Mayor of Belfast

1. I don't usually make New Year's resolutions, and I certainly have never got into the habit of new millennium resolutions! However, I hope we can get a lot of resolutions in our city.

2. I lead an unhealthy lifestyle, therefore I would like to change this by doing more exercise and eating a more balanced diet.

3. Jubilee 2000 is my great hope globally, i.e. that unfair debts from third world nations will be cancelled, thereby allowing those countries to develop economically and politically.

Jack Bourke, Mayor of Limerick

1. In this, my 33rd year in public life, I will continue to endeavour to do the impossible for many of my constituents. I will continue to remind those who have no desire to live up to their obligations that everything starts inside our own hall door. I can assure you this does not make me popular.

2. I don't smoke, I do everything else in modera-

tion, I think, I am not a paragon. I should play more golf, I should cut the grass more often, I can't think of anything I want to give up. "Oh, would the power the gift to give us, to see ourselves as others see us." *R Burns*.

3. I aspire to becoming a Senator, I have tried on four occasions and been pipped at the post. I dream and hope and pray for peace on this island and will be disappointed if it doesn't happen in my time. Sure it only requires a number of lunatices (on all sides) to take the cure.

Councillor Senator Joe Doyle, Lord Mayor of Dublin, 1998-1999

1. In my last position as Chairman of the Regional Authority, I participated in a study of the Dublin economy, a study that set out to establish the strengths and weaknesses of the economy. While the strengths of the public economy are obvious to all, the growth in employment results in improved spending power for our citizens also has the benefit of increasing exchequer returns. Nevertheless, there are many weaknesses in the Dublin economy and there are still many areas of social exclusion and deprivation.

   When you examine these areas, one is frightened to find that many young people leave our education system at the age of fifteen or sixteen. Ballymun is a good example of this, where over 52 per cent of the population leave school at fifteen. The majority of young people who leave school at this age have no qualification for life and easily fall into the habit of taking drugs, which in itself is a form of escapism from the reality of life. Many of these young people had the benefit of remedial teachers at the primary level, but unfortunately in our secondary education system there is no provision for remedial teaching that will encourage young people to stay on at school. We need teachers who can enable them to overcome the difficulties they are experiencing in their second educational level so that they will remain in education until they are eighteen years of age and qualified with a leaving certificate.

If I was privileged to have a millennium resolution that would have an enriching effect, it would be addressed to this area of our education system, especially for young people who come from areas of social exclusion and deprivation. I long for an education system that would encourage them to stay in school until they were eighteen years of age so that they would possess some qualifications that would enrich them for a better standard of living.

2. While the Irish economy has benefited tremendously well from the Urban Renewal Programme, which was first established in 1987, as I stated in my first reply, there remains many areas of social exclusion and deprivation. While tax relief to the whole country has amounted to £3 billion for the Urban Renewal Programme and £500 million of this has been spent in Dublin, nevertheless the main beneficiaries of Urban Re-

newal have been developers, builders and the owners of inner city apartments. It cannot besaid often enough that this has helped to improve the infrastructure of the city, but unfortunately local communities have not benefited. The Department of the Environment is now introducing a new approach under Integrated Area Programmes. Dublin Corporation has selected five areas in the city for this purpose and 23 per cent tax relief, which was available right across the city in the Urban Renewal Programme, will now be only available in these selected areas. It is hoped that from this process that local communities will benefit from Urban Renewal and this will remove the impoverishing effect that has underlined these communities.

3. Personally: peace in Ireland. Globally: better understanding of man's inhumanity to man.

Chapter 9

POLITICALLY CORRECT

Bertie Ahern, *An Taoiseach*

1. On a personal basis I want to try and find some quiet time in my week where I can reflect on the major issues of the moment. I do have my early morning jogging time but that is really a physical workout and waking-up to the new day. And then at the weekend I try to give as much time as possible to reading the mountain of government briefs which must be gone through carefully.

   So while I don't intend in any way becoming a hermit, I will seek out a little more calm and a little more space to consider and ponder long-term national strategies.

2. It is interesting how the words 'giving up' strike a different chord with different people in such strikingly diverse ways. From boyhood I have held to the custom of 'giving up' something during November for the Holy Souls and during Lent in memory of Christ's sacrifices.

   Then it used to be sweets or lemonade, now it's drink, and apart from any religious significance, I don't think it does the body any harm to give it a break from alcohol for four or five weeks at a time.

   Apart from that I would always be naturally

inclined 'to do' extra activities rather than 'give up' anything else, and by doing those things to widen my perspective, to show greater appreciation or to reflect more deeply on the needs of others.

3. Well, I am writing these comments as I make my final preparations to go up to the North of Ireland during Easter Week for the second year in a row. In 1998 we managed to forge together the historic Good Friday Agreement. This year we seek to unlock its wonderful potential by using the magic key of compromise, if all the parties can dig deep enough to find that key, in mutual respect, trust and generosity. I don't think there is any greater legacy that we can pass on to our children than an Ireland united in peaceful co-operation, with every person on the island having the right to attain their individual dreams and aspirations without let or hindrance.

   I dream that the city I love will be transformed into a city of beautiful homes, classy public buildings, top-class facilities and excellent job opportunities, with a fast modern transport system, while still maintaining that special spirit of craic and enjoyment.

   On a personal level I just hope to make as good a contribution as I can to my city and country, and then quietly make way for my successor. Serving is a privilege, and I have been blessed in my opportunities.

Nuala Ahern, MEP

1. My vision for a new millennium would be to seriously examine the roots of human violence in an individual family and in a social and national context and to really have faith that human beings can move away from domination and violence in their relationships with each other and the world. As a public representative I believe women can make a difference in our concepts and beliefs about violence and its roots as causes of many of the problems of our world. I believe that this is so serious and deep-seated a human dilemma that I want to make it the focus of my own personal resolutions to examine my habits of relationships in family life and in public life for the seeds of the kind of domination which I believe lead to violence.

2. The second millennium has been a period of increasing human control and incredible achievements in technology. This has, however, gone hand in hand with a philosophy of dominance that was often imposed with great violence against women, against other races or in destruction of the earth.

3. My vision has been inspired by meeting with women from Bosnia, Croatia and Serbia (all states of former Yugoslavia) who have experienced dreadful violence and who have made common cause with others, such as those women in Northern Ireland who have resisted violence in their own communities.

Brian Crowley, MEP

1. To work towards bringing people together and focus on the real celebration of the millennium.

2. Impatience.

3. On a personal level, to keep up my optimistic outlook on life, and to help to change the world to make it a better place. Globally, that we can create a greater understanding that the different traditions and cultures around the world can be the concrete that binds us together, not the divisive force that some people would like to make them.

Austin Currie, TD

1. To spend less time reading newspapers, particularly on Sundays, and give more time to reading books.

2. Answering stupid questions.

3. Personally: to survive as long as I am mentally alert. Globally: flowering of the Northern Ireland Peace Process to the benefit of people in the Irish isle.

Mildred Fox, TD

1. To exercise a little more and to slow down and take in more of my surroundings.

2. My untidy streak. I am one of these people whose room looks upside down to the untrained eye. Only I know where everything is, and go berserk if anyone tidies my room. Maybe if I was tidier nobody would touch anything belonging to me.

3. Personally: for Wicklow to win the All-Ireland. Globally: for mankind to stop murdering one another, be they street thugs or super-powers. Life is precious.

Tony Gregory, Independent TD

1. To do all the things I wanted to do over the last twenty years but did not get time to do.

2. Worrying about the next election.

3. To continue in good health well into the next millennium. To get a little hideaway in the mountains to escape from the pressures of political activism. To see a more caring approach to our environment.

Mary Hanafin, TD

1. To make time for family and friends – the really important people in life.

2. I won't give up but will take up more exercise.

3. Personally: health and happiness. Globally: peace and co-existence.

Liam Hyland, MEP

1. To help in any way I can to promote continuing economic and social development in our country within the agreed framework of Agenda 2000, and with particular emphasis on employment, the elimination of drugs and a fairer distribution of wealth on a regional basis.

2. As I move towards retirement, I would like to take life a little easier and give more time to my family.

3. To seek a realisation of my aspirations for Rural Development with particular emphasis on the survival of small rural towns and villages, including the retention of the maximum number of farm families and with emphasis on the environment and its preservation for society.

Donal J Lydon, Senator

1. To continue to fight against the evil of abortion.

2. To resist – to some extent – the joys of Italian food!

3. That abortion would be banned totally in every country in the world forever.

Bernie Malone, MEP

1. To leave plenty of time before flights. To live in an orderly environment by discarding old papers, clothes, etc., and to get the house decorated for the first time since we moved in the 70s.

2. I would like to give up making resolutions which I never keep. I would like to develop a more positive attitude and be slower to criticise.

3. Personally: to continue my work and service for Dubliners and for all European citizens and that my efforts will be guided by principles of justice and equality. Globally: that we must all continue to strive for a global ethic to ensure peace and dignity for people everywhere.

Liz McManus, TD

1. Work smarter, not harder. Lighten up. See the wood for the trees. Hold my head up high. Worry less. Sleep more. Enjoy.

2. After 51 years of living with my traits, I wouldn't part with any of them.

3. Personal: to stay alive. Global: to live in a world governed by humanity in which each person has the opportunity to realise his/her potential as equals and in environment that breathes freely.

David Norris, Senator

1. My millennium resolution is to attempt at last to conquer my ghastly combination of bad driving, road rage and general automobile irritation and to display the kind of courtesy on the road that I expect from others.

2. A personal trait I would like to give up is self-indulgence.

3. Personally: to spend more time on my domestic life with Ezra in our apartment in Jerusalem and to try my hand seriously at creative writing. Globally: I would hope for a resolution of the many tragic situations in the world, in places such as Tibet and East Timor, and for the human race at last to wake up to the consequences of its greed and savagery, both for fellow humans and for the animals, who are rapidly becoming extinct, and for the environment generally.

Anne Ormond, Senator

1. To have good health and have a better quality of life.

2. Anxiety.

3. Health, happiness and satisfaction with one's lifestyle.

Albert Reynolds, TD and Former Taoiseach

1. Peace with justice in Northern Ireland.

2. All violence, conflict, hatred and sectarian bigotry in Northern Ireland.

3. Good health for my wife and family.

Gerry Steadman, Communications Manager at the Department of Health and Children

1. To see as much of it as I can and be able to spell it right up to the end!

2. Pessimism to go out with the old millennium and optimism to come in with the new.

3. Personally: to be healthy and happy, and that goes double for my children, Adam and Leah! Globally: the end of the 20th century has seen

major advances in information and computer technology. It would be nice if the new millennium could complement these advances with new and improved methods of developing the power of the mind. Given that we use such a small amount of the brain's capacity, we obviously still have a lot to learn.

Chapter 10

INTERNATIONAL INFLUENCE

United Kingdom: Veronica Sutherland,
Former British Ambassador to Ireland

1. Globally, I most sincerely wish for peace throughout the world, especially here in Ireland.

Israel: Zvi Gabay,
Former Ambassador to Ireland

1. Personally, my hope for the new millennium is tolerance between people in general, and between Jews and Arabs in particular. We all wish for peaceful co-existence between Israel, the Arab countries surrounding Israel and beyond.

2. Peace and tolerance will provide us with the incentives to work together to solve the problems facing humanity in general and in the Middle East. These in the main are protecting the ecology, providing sufficient food and water and providing decent living for all the people living on the earth.

Republic of Bulgaria: Peter Poptchev, Charge d' Affaires at the Bulgarian Embassy in Ireland

1. Consultation and co-ordination at all levels.

2. Thinking and acting petty.

3. Attaining sufficiency, both personally and globally.

South Africa: P R Dietrichsen, Former Ambassador to Ireland

1. My resolution will be to keep more regular contact with friends and family and to resume contact where I have lost contact.

2. I shall probably resolve to temper my ambitions – not give it up as a trait, but to balance it more with quality of life, etc.

3. A dream I have is for the African continent to become prosperous and happy again; for disease, poverty, crime and violence to be eradicated. Personally I would be happy to have a healthy and peaceful life with my family, to enjoy sport and some quality free time.

USA: Earle Scarlett, Deputy Chief of Mission at the United States Embassy

1. Be a better husband and father.

2. Become more open-minded.

3. To ensure that my children have fulfiling experiences and become productive citizens. Globally, in my and my wife's professional lives, work towards making the environment more peaceful and help the US in its efforts to do so.

Chapter 11

MIXING WITH THE MEDIA

Kim Bielenberg, Journalist

1. Ambition is said to be the last refuge of the failure, so I will not worry about that. My resolution is to outlive the driving test, which I fail regularly. Apparently, there will be a self-drive car in operation by the year 2015. I also resolve to give up reading newspapers and watching television.

2. Absent-mindedness. I have lost this piece of paper three times. I lost my friend's bicycle. I am determined not to lose my car.

3. My dream is that my son and daughter are happy, peace continues in the North and Ireland wins the World Cup.

Jonathon Philbin Bowman

1. I tend not to believe in resolutions, or rather, I tend not to believe in my ability to keep them, probably because we are all used to framing resolutions in absolute terms: "I will never...", "I think always...", or "Three times a week...". So then we fail, we give up. Instead I prefer to think in terms of aspirations, and of better ways of

being in and about the world. And so if we want a kinder world, we must be kinder. That includes being kind to yourself, and kind to yourself when you fail to be kind to others. Or when you fail to be as kind as you might like to be. Do unto yourself, perhaps, as you would have others do unto you.

2. One of the people who I find most inspiring, and fun, used to be called Richard Alpert. That was before he was slung out of Harvard for taking too many mind-altering substances along with his colleague Timothy Leary. Now he is called Ram Dass. Recently he said something along these lines: "I've done it all now, the spiritual practice, for something like forty years. The meditation, the chanting, the acid, working with the dying. The silent retreats, the fasting, the monasteries. And do you know in all that time I don't think I've lost one of the neurotic, Jewish, annoying traits in my personality. I'm still critical, still judgmental, I still have lust. But I'm not so attached to them. I sort of say, 'ah, lust, how are you, come in here my old friend, sit down, have a cup of tea'." You can get hold of tapes of Ram Dass in bookstores.

As for traits, I think the thing I would most like to let go of would be terrible impatience. Not because I seem rude or impatient to others, but because it drives me mad, too. My son reminds me of this. Right now we are on holiday in France, but even before we landed he was asking when we could go somewhere else, like maybe London.

3. The first person I ever interviewed was Quentin Crisp. I think I was about sixteen. Last year I went back to New York and interviewed him in the Copper Square Café where he has lunch, religiously, every day. We were joined by a young man from London who seemed agitated in his search for answers. He asked Quentin urgently what was the purpose of life. "The purpose of life," Crisp replied, "is happiness." And what is the secret of happiness, asked the young man, even more urgently. Crisp paused – I think we had moved to a hub at this point. "The secret of happiness," he said after a pause, "is to remain in the present moment, in your mind, and your body, for as long as is humanly possible."

As for the world? Remain in awe. Read. Think for yourself. Celebrate. Remember that anthropologists are people too. It is far better to accumulate inspiration and insight than to carve rules in stone. When flying, remember that the aisles are the windows of the soul, especially if the air hostess is beautiful. Moods are like the weather: they change. Awaken. Grow. And respect your youngers and worsers, as well as you elders and betters. At the end of our days we will be judged by love alone. Good luck, now. And be not afraid.

Finally there's the story my friend Catherine Ingram tells about a six-year-old who asked her the following: "Pretend that you are in a clearing in the jungle. Suddenly you are surrounded by hungry tigers. What do you do?"

"I don't know," Catherine said. "I might climb

p a tree."

"There are no trees in the clearing," said the six-year-old. Catherine thought some more. "I know what I would do," said the kid.

"What?" asked Catherine.

"I would stop pretending."

Gay Byrne, Broadcaster

1. To enjoy each day to the full.

2. Fussing.

3. To treat life as one long holiday and to become a computer guru. Peace and an end to violence, hunger and pain in an environmentally friendly planet.

Martina Devlin, Journalist

1. To have a work of fiction published that I can be proud of.

2. Self-doubt and negativity.

3. To be settled in a new home with the prospect of staying there long-term (it'll make a change). Globally, for the Good Friday Agreement to be fully and inclusively operational.

Eamon Dunphy, Journalist and Broadcaster

1. Stop squandering time and money.

2. Optimism.

3. To live happily and peacefully. Peace and plenty for everyone.

Garrett Harte, Series Producer 20/20, TV3

1. I am not very good at keeping to New Year resolutions but my hope is that this year I will be able to make more time for my family and friends. In the last couple of years my job has demanded more time of me which unfortunately reflects on the lack of time I have for friends. Going back home to Donegal more often will also be an important element of my resolution.

2. I am one of a family of smokers that talk more about giving up than actually making a concerted effort to do something serious about it. To give up smoking is by far the most challenging test of my willpower, but I have trust in my continued hope of success.

3. Personally, I believe there is a need for my generation to develop a more transparent, mature society. The decline we are now experiencing in relation to the Church, banks and past governments have all contributed to the lack of leadership that any good country deserves.

Having been brought up in a highly political family and raised along the border, my aspiration for the next millennium is that we can develop a society on the island of Ireland whereby all citizens, regardless of religion, race or colour, can accommodate each other. To be regarded as a prosperous country does not only refer to material wealth but also to richness in tolerance, cultural diversity and trust.

I count myself as having had a very privileged and enjoyable upbringing that gave me a great platform for life. I hope that more and more children will also be afforded an opportunity like I had.

Lorna Hogg, Journalist

1. To be more open; to try more, to travel, work and learn more and different skills. To experiment more – with foods, new ideas, philosophies, meeting new people. To be less judgmental and more relaxed – and above all, to have more fun.

2. Worry – 90 per cent useless and unnecessary. Control – to learn to go with the process of life. Preparation – useful, but constricting. Waiting for everything to be completed, before having fun/moving to another task – things are never completed! Regret – it's true – your main regret is the things you didn't do. Over conscientiousness – sometimes 'good enough' really is.

3. Dreams – that Nostrodamus was wrongly read, and the end of the world as we know it isn't nigh on December 31st! That mankind can develop a better framework politically or through an existing link to understand international conflict, and be able to ease escalating international tension.

    That mankind can cut down on global warming, and reduce the effects already in force.

    That I become a healthier, wealthier and happier person – with the time and energy to use these attributes in some productive way aside from myself.

Síle McArdle, Journalist and Sub-Editor

1. I don't make New Year's resolutions any more as I believe they create pressure to perform. Life is difficult enough without pitting yourself against yourself in that way. However, I do make general plans throughout the year depending on what's happening and in that regard my 2000 resolution is to allow myself to be unconditionally happy.

2. Worrying about the future.

3. My personal overriding aspiration is for a blissfully aware state of acceptance of each and every moment as a part of a grand plan, which I must trust implicitly. Globally, rather than wishing for general things like world peace and an end to famine and natural disaster – which sadly are

unrealistic aspirations – I wish that state of bliss and enlightenment for every single other person in the world, whoever they are.

Lara McMillan, Journalist

1. Treat others as you would like them to treat you.

2. Insecurity and excess baggage.

3. To continue to appreciate true love. Tolerance all around.

Celine Naughton, Editor, Woman's Way

1. Somebody once told me that for the New Year, she resolved to devote one day a month to herself, and I think that's such a charming idea, I'd like to adopt it for the millennium. It can be hard to juggle the various roles of wife, mother, daughter, sister, friend, editor and so on, and make time for myself. Mind you, the only one stopping me doing that is me, but like so many women, I would find it indulgent to announce, "This is my day", and make them all go away while I have a manicure, a bath and read a book or whatever. Still, it's tempting! I don't really make New Year's resolutions, though, even if it is a millennium, because I'm just not that disciplined and they're bound to be broken.

2. Physically, I'm a bit lazy. I try to exercise regularly, but I'd always hop on a bus rather than walk, or find excuses not to go for a cycle after work – it's dark when I get home or I'm tired. I'd also like to just be a better person – give everyone the benefit of the doubt, do good works, not be cynical and always be good-humoured. But even as I say this, I think, "Yeah, in an ideal world". I'd like to be able to say no whenever I want, but in the interests of balance, one often needs to compromise. I'd like to lose a couple of stone in weight as well. Oh, and if I could lose those phobias – dentist, public speaking and spiders – my life would be perfect!

3. I'll be 40 in the year 2000. From the time I was a teenager, I'd looked forward to my thirties because I saw it as a time when you got your act together, had more experience and confidence and knew who you were. This was confirmed to me in reality. I've been blessed with a happy marriage and two beautiful daughters whom I love dearly. In my forties, I hope for an even deeper sense of those things I aspired to in my thirties. I embrace the wisdom, understanding and maturity which I think comes with age. Globally, I can't help thinking of John Lennon's classic song, 'Imagine', as the ultimate dream. Well, it's a possibility, if we could only stop fighting with each other.

   Technology has opened up new possibilities we never thought possible. In this millennium, we've had two world wars, an industrial revolution, a social revolution and now a technological revolution. All sorts of avenues are open to us with this experience and information, and which road we take is up to us as human beings. I am not a believer in organised religion, though I see where it had a place in the past, and I'm encouraged to see a new kind of spirituality coming on stream – a voyage of discovery of parts of the mind we have not yet tapped into combined with a true appreciation of other plants and animals and every living thing. If this is married with the technology available to us, it could lead us to a wonderful world, where countries and individuals are united, where difference is valued and discrimination, hunger, poverty, injustice, hatred and war are all things of the past. Imagine!

"Navan Man", Radio Personality

1. Stop cooking my own socks. Get a big saucepan, boil the shit out of them until they boil over.

2. To endeavour to give up cooking my socks.

3. Getting a whole load of chickens – as many as I can between now and the end of the year and cooking them. Peace, success, give the six counties back and then send them home to Scotland to live in John Bruton's holiday home.

Larissa Nolan, Journalist

1. My resolution is to get fit. Do more exercise – do some exercise at least!

2. Stop worrying. Stop losing my temper so easily.

3. Personally: just to be well and happy and to live for the moment. Globally: a united Ireland.

Paddy O'Shea, Freelance Journalist

1. To concentrate on maximising my resources and potential creative project to capitalise on the current Celtic tiger economy.

2. My addiction to television soaps which are pointless and time-wasting. The time could be better utilised pursuing creative projects or developing my intellect surfing the Net.

3. To find elusive happiness through self-fulfilment and the pursuit of spiritual well being, and to balance that with the joy of materialism in the ever-changing world of electronics.

Helen Shaw, Director of Radio, RTÉ

1. To grow old in body only!

2. Impatience and intolerance!

3. That Ireland grows into a more confident, caring and self-possessed country, both north and south.

Ryan Tubridy, RTÉ Journalist
and Radio Presenter

1. To increase my boredom threshold while learning to appreciate the good things that tend to happen without you realising it.

2. Impatience, excessive approach to things and a tendency to bore...

3. Contentment for my family, tolerance on a global scale would be nice...dream on!

Jan Van Embden, Senior Reporter,
Bray People

1. Live long and prosper!

2. Addiction to *Star Trek*.

3. To be comfortable and happy – personally and globally.

Anna, Journalist

1. Less smoking, less drinking and a slimmer bottom (the same as every other year)!

2. Being paranoid.

3. To be able to buy a house in Dublin for under £100,000.

Damien, Journalist

1. To travel the world – get out of this God forsaken country, for a while anyway.

2. Saying I will travel when I don't. Grumbling about Ireland because it is not worth it.

3. To own a house.

Josephine, Journalist

1. To get healthy and remain content without chasing an unreasonable utopia. To make more time for good friends.

2. Nail-biting and smoking. Become less selfish with my time. Become less trusting.

3. To continue enjoying my work, relationships and family. Like every aspiring Miss World, I would like to see a real global effort to end hunger and famine. Also, a united and peaceful Ireland.

Chapter 12

ECCLESIASTICAL EXPRESSIONS

Bishop Barden, Former Archbishop of Isfahan of the Latins

1. Faith, love and hope are all in the waiting.

2. Others know that.

3. Looking forward to the next life. God's love will embrace all humanity.

Bishop Brendan Comiskey, Bishop of Ferns

1. To be more conscious of what it is to be Christian.

2. I don't think it helpful to work on 'giving up'. I would rather aim at living out what it means to be a follower of Christ.

3. Personally: to recapture in my own life the vision of Christ and to live it out more faithfully. Nationally: to see more soul in the Celtic tiger. Globally: cancellation of third world debt.

Brian Coogan, CSSP, Priest

1. To be kind.

2. Forgetfulness.

3. To enjoy good health, peace in Ireland, justice in the Third World.

Sean Copeland, Pastor,
Southside Vineyard Christian Fellowship

1. I don't make New Year's resolutions. I have a list of goals, which I live by daily.

2. As a Christian, I want my life to mirror that of Jesus. Everything else I'd like to give up.

3. I'd like to see a change from the lopsided economic monopolies of the rich to a more balanced world economy which respects and values human rights for all.

Bishop Joseph Duffy, Bishop of Clogher

1. My resolution for the millennium is to strive with renewed emphasis to live the Christian life in a way that relates better to the changed world we live in.

   Life, especially human life, is a gift – a one-way gift with no strings attached other than to receive it and to acknowledge it adequately. That is my understanding of Eucharist, daily Eucharist which transcends passing moods and daily concerns. The permanent appropriate attitude is thanks.

   An attitude of thanks helps to restore the zest for living. That I have been given the gift of life means that I am loved by God, that I am trusted, that I am held in high esteem, not for what I do or have, but for what I am.

   Because the source of life never runs dry, in spite of passing years, I have undying hope. No matter what happens or fails to happen, no matter who offends of ignores me, the future is always bright.

2. I am not sure that it is possible to give up personal traits at the age of 65. I would see this question rather as looking at myself for blind spots, for qualities which I take for granted but which need attention. On reflection – and it's hard to be definite about this – I think that these are mostly in the area of communication. I find it difficult, for example, to evaluate human experience in the way that best helps myself and others. This may be about sharing information,

ideas, opinions and convictions. But it's more often about making a constructive response to individual needs, in words or deeds.

3. My dream and aspiration for the world of the new millennium is increased recognition and appreciation of the dignity of every human person. The development of human rights in the second half of the 20th century, the anti-apartheid movement, the ecumenical impulse in the churches, solidarity with the developing world, equal rights for women, the campaign against abortion, conflict resolution and peace-keeping, attention to better medical care and social services for all citizens: these are some of the existing expressions of concern for human dignity which augur well for the future.

This impetus towards greater respect for human dignity, in order to be authentic and lasting, needs to be based on an adequate philosophy of the human person. This means that more attention must be paid to the mystical dimension, to the hidden depths of the human psyche, to the insights of poetry and the arts, to the hallowed and well-ordered values of indigenous culture and tradition. The education system in every country, including our own, must make more time for the humanities and for personal development.

As a Christian, one prays for a more radical and purified acceptance of the message of Jesus. The Christian way of life is now seen more as a series of free choices than a set programme, more as a journey on the open road than on a railway track. This is a welcome development but it demands continual renewal on the part of those who have already chosen Jesus Christ. In the economically successful Western world in which we now live in Ireland, it looks as if numbers going to church will continue to fall; but, while this is regrettable, it will be compensated for by the dedication of those who continue to go, as well as by the rediscovery of the dynamism of the Spirit working in human hearts, conforming them to the likeness of Christ.

Personally speaking, my deepest desire has nothing to do with the new millennium, except insofar as it marks the final phase of my own life on the planet. The daily struggle to meet God is a down-to-earth business from which there is no escape. The most challenging aspect of the struggle is its utter simplicity. Because it concerns mainly God and not me, my feelings, likes and dislikes may be an occasional help or hindrance, but ultimately they have nothing to do with the purpose of the exercise. The temptation is to pay lip service, to wave God as a banner, to fall into step with the crowd. With people rather than with God it's easier to get by. Years of experience enable us to cope with boredom, embarrassments and the various forms of distress we encounter. But with God it is different. There are no social skills to be tapped here, no honest means of avoiding Him, no valid reasons to be less than happy in His company. He wants my regular attention that I might live always in His presence. The desire – and the resolution – is to give Him what He wants.

Gerry French, Priest and Director,
Irish Emigrant Chaplancy

1. To be more true to myself – meaning that I reflect more on what are my real true desires – that I try and become the person I was intended to be in the last millennium.

2. Being distracted easily and not focused. To give up workaholism.

3. To become physically fit – to look after the body in the sedentary, electronic new millennium. I would hope to be independent enough to keep my friends and not become dependent on them. That Ireland would own its emigrants and that I would play a part in that. Globally: world debt to be worked on, ecology issues to become paramount, or there'll be no globe!!

Reverend David J Kerr, President,
Methodist Church of Ireland (Belfast)

1. To live in the global village, open to and appreciative of the richness of the diversity of the human family.

2. Living my life by crisis management.

3. After 40 years of ministry, to retire with health to enjoy family, friends and developing new interests. That the new millennium may see the nations learning to co-operate rather than compete and everyone learning when enough is enough in their material possessions.

Jack McArdle, Priest of
Sacred Hearts Congregation and Writer

1. To grow old gracefully, one day at a time, with a sense of gratitude for the gifts of each day.

2. I would love dearly to give up a need to be in the limelight and to be more at ease with a simpler and more humble approach to life, to situations and to people.

3. A greater division of the world's wealth, so that all people could access the benefits – food, health, education, etc.

Chapter 13

HELPING HANDS

Rolande Anderson, Assistant Director, Rutland Centre

1. To continue to live every day to the full, but to devote more leisure time to my family and friends.

2. I would like to be a little less conscientious and to worry less about what the future holds.

3. Personally: to spend more time with my wife, Barbara, and to see our children grow up happy and healthy and to accomplish their dreams. To travel and to play more golf. To write more, to be in a job position that will further allow me to influence government policy on addictions. Globally: more tolerance for differences. Greater awareness about the environment. Reductions in the use of alcohol and mind-altering drugs. Less aggression and violence.

Olive Braiden, Director,
Dublin Rape Crisis Centre

1. To give more time and energy to enjoy the company of the important people in my life.

2. My propensity to burn the candle at both ends.

3. Personally: that women be valued for their real contribution at every level of society worldwide, which in turn will lead to the elimination of the appalling worldwide violence against women. Globally: that Ireland would be a place of welcome and refuge for people forced to leave their own countries. That a creative and workable solution be found for world hunger.

Rosaleen Fadden, Director, Ionad Folláin
(Centre of Wholeness)

1. To be more aware of the earth's condition and to be more sensitive to caring for it.

2. Narcissism. Navel-gazing.

3. Personally: to have more fun – to dance and sing more. Joy to the world. Globally: to enjoy the world we live in and to treat it gently.

Joe Gallagher, Teacher and Voluntary Director, The Dublin Samaritans

1. Resolutions: to do a health food cookery course and make more time for reading.

2. Personal traits: wasting energy on things over which I have no control.

3. Dreams and aspirations: personally, to aim to become a more rounded person in mind, body and spirit. Globally, that there will continue to be a greater awareness of the separate needs of others, particularly the less fortunate in society.

Jennifer Guinness, Former Chairperson, Victim Support

1. To spend more time with my grandchildren, my boat and my garden.

2. Fussing, worrying about things I can't change.

3. Personally: to travel to wild and beautiful places. Globally: for mankind to stop damaging and destroying irreplaceable wildlife and for all ethnic and religious bigotry to stop.

Dr Mary Redmond, Solicitor, Patron and Former Director, Irish Hospice Foundation

1. To achieve a greater balance in my life.

2. Working ridiculously long hours; worrying about things that are not going to happen until tomorrow; being content with little exercise.

3. Personally: to increase the amount of time I spend on the inner self; to reread the great writers of the past and perhaps to tackle Camus in French! To pursue soul as a complement to the changes the millennium will certainly bring. Globally: I hope the millennium kick starts the desire to revisit existing structures, institutions and ideas and brings about a change mentality. There must be a fresh commitment to respecting human rights and more than ever before an innovative approach by all parties to ensure that human life is lived and cared for in the best possible way.

Bridget Shannon, Social Worker

1. Fall madly in love!

2. A fine human being; free from materialism.

3. Personally: I'd like to stay alive to experience peace in Ireland. Globally: renewed reverence for God, for spirituality of the great traditions of religious belief. Dignity of the human person and life.

Focus Ireland

Moira Patricia Bowers, Receptionist, The Sanctuary, Stanhope Green

1. To live in joy, receptivity of the highest good for me, gratitude, openness and trust. To experience light, levity, love and laughter.

2. Anxiety, panic, sadness, spiritual deafness.

3. Personally: to maintain good health. To have enough money to live on, plus some. To write a bestseller. To have a permanent love-partner (of mind, body and spirit match). To live in a detached villa-style house, joyfully, gratefully, thus benefiting both myself and others, by hospitality and grace. Globally: to be part of making a difference, assisting in bringing peace, love, wellbeing, harmony and light to the world.

Noel Forde, Receptionist, Housing Division

1. To help the poor just as I was helped.

2. Smoking and drinking.

3. World peace and no more homelessness.

Sister Stanislaus Kennedy,
Irish Sister of Charity, Founder and
Life President of Focus Ireland

1. To become what I pray for – grateful, gracious, compassionate, hope-filled, peace-filled and loving, and to share these gifts with all my brothers and sisters.

2. Any traits of ingratitude, because every approach of life is a gift, all that is given and all that is not given.

3. That in Ireland we would carry out a referendum where we would vote for an Ireland that is just, fair and caring, an Ireland where nobody is in want amongst us. That this decision would be implemented fully by all of us before the end of the first decade and as such, become the people we are, people of 'good will', a shining example to the whole world.

   That the rich nations of the world would share their human and material resources generously with the poorer nations, and that we in the rich nations would learn from the generosity of the poorer nations.

   That world debts would be cancelled and that the United Nations would be given more authority and support to bring about a more just and peaceful world.

   The millennium is a time of jubilee and liberation, and I pray and hope that we will all find it in our hearts to make the words of Deuteronomy, Chapter 15 verse 4, come true in the first decade of the new millennium: "Let there be no poor among you, do not harden your heart or close your hand against those poor brothers (and sisters) of yours but be open handed with them and lend them enough for their needs and with them free you must not let them go."

My dream for the millennium is that it would be a time of sharing generously with each other, with our families, with our community, with our society and with the whole universe. That it would be a time for forgiveness, to forgive everything we can, forgive each other, forgive trespasses, forgive sins, forgive family, forgive world debt, forgive the impossible. For it is the unforgivable forgiven that makes us whole.

Therese Kennelly, Project Leader

1. To continue to live and be happy and healthy again. To try and expand upon my present job.

2. Being too critical of both myself and others.

3. Start a family. Move west of Ireland. World peace to be achieved. Greater equality in the distribution of wealth.

Focus Ireland's
Stanhope Green Tenants

Tenant

1. Don't know.

2. Not think as much.

3. Enjoy life more. Get a job.

Tenant

2. Smoking, drinking, working hard for slave money.

3. My own would be to get a good paid job and be off long-term unemployment assistance. Better facilities in Eastern Health Board where I am based.

Tenant

1. To be able to give up the cigarettes.

2. People who are always late annoy me.

3. To have peace of mind and a better life.

Tenant

1. To have peace of mind. To help others and have little time for myself.

2. To be less selfish. To have more patience with other people.

3. To be in employment or else to be in further education.

Tenant

1. My resolution will be to try and get on better with people and not eat as much chocolates.

2. I would like to give up smoking.

3. Personally, I would like to start a course and meet new people. Globally, I would like to see peace in our country especially up the North.

Tenant

1. To be able to give up cigarettes.

2. No patience.

3. Peace in our country and peace of mind.

Tenant

1. Help the homeless more.

2. Drugs, gambling, smoking, etc.

3. Peace in Northern Ireland.

Tenant

1. Have a job.

2. Stop stealing.

3. I would like to have my own home and start up a business and peace and no more drugs.

Anonymous Social Worker, Northwestern Health Board

1. Not sure if I am interested in the millennium per se. Get fitter. Sing more.

2. Tendency to put things on the long finger.

3. Personally: keep learning. Globally: not give up on working for peace. Wake up to environment issues.

Chapter 14

ARTISTS ARRIVE

Jim Bartley, Actor, 'Bella' in *Fair City*

1. To be available to people.

2. Not to be so selfish.

3. To be able to relax, have a pint, back a few horses and not to feel guilty. More help for the under-privileged. Create more funds to help those suffering mentally, physically and emotionally.

Philip Carty, Composer

1. Improve discipline in my life, both spiritually and physically.

2. Temptation.

3. Personally: for my children to say, "That was my Daddy." Globally: for people to reflect on the simplicity of life 2000 years ago.

Paddy Cole, Jazz Player

1. To try and make Ireland a cleaner place to live. I really hate to see all the litter in our country.

2. I'm a bit of a television addict. I'd like to give up watching so much television.

3. That there is peace and happiness all over the world.

Kevin Ferguson, Singer (Tenor)

1. To be more charitable.

2. Impatience.

3. To fulfil my ambition to be one of the great operatic tenors. I would like to see my children grow up in a world where the threat of war ceases to exist.

John B Keane, Writer

1. Redouble my efforts to point out the use of violence to solve problems.

2. Lack of clarity at times and reluctance to speak out when it should be heard.

3. Peace all over and peace in my home.

Sonny Knowles, Singer

1. Staying alive as long as I can.

2. Not to worry so much.

3. Personally: have all my family with me together. Globally: end of war and religious differences.

Andre Laurent, Sculpture Student

1. Be really productive. To make a lot of money on 31 December 1999 – there will be a lot of people willing to pay obscene amounts of money for staff, childminders, anything.

2. Vanity, laziness.

3. Get fit, money, fame, money, a house, a husband, a dog, learn to make pancakes and crochet.

Giles Lury, Author

1. To live life to the full as I won't be here for the next millennium (3000)!

2. My lack of patience.

3. Personally: to achieve a better balance between my work and home life. Globally: to see people live and let live.

Niamh O'Brien, Singer (Soprano)

1. To use my gift as a singer to its full potential.

2. Intolerance.

3. To be a respected singer and provide a stable and nurturing family home. That food, medicine and shelter be available to anybody who needs it.

Daniel O'Donnell, Singer

1. I'm not one for New Year's resolutions so I don't think I will be making any this year, either.

2. By times I'm a little quick-tempered. I would like to control that.

3. Personally, I just hope my life can continue as it is. I've been very fortunate. Globally (like many others, I'm sure!), I'd like to see an end to the pain and suffering of so many people in the world caused by war and famine.

Lisa O'Sullivan, Artist

1. To work with people using my art to relieve hurt – art therapy.

2. To become more confident with people.

3. Peace in Ireland. Forgiveness between people in Ireland and England. I'd love to work with my art in a half-way house.

Janet Pierce, Artist

1. To concentrate more on the spiritual side of life.

2. The tendency to doubt that all works for good.

3. A dream of harmony in all aspects of life and equality between the first and third worlds.

Maureen Potter, Actress

1. As my New Year's resolutions usually only last as far as my birthday on 3 January, I don't think I'll even bother for the millennium.

2. To stop shouting at obtrusive chairmen on television discussion programmes when they interrupt someone in full flow. So far Paxman and Bowman have ignored me, so why persist?

3. Globally: I pray that Bono and company succeed in getting the huge debts of poor countries written off. Maybe we have a few ex-Taosigh who could tell them how to do it.

Simon Ryan, Painter

1. To stage a play for charity for deaf children.

2. Smoking.

3. For a drama group I'm involved with to reach the All Ireland finals in Athlone.

Alice Taylor, Writer

1. To plant a wood of gingko trees.

2. Saying yes when I really want to say no. Being impetuous at certain times.

3. Litter-free Ireland. Cottage in a wood where I could hear the dawn chorus every morning.

Gavin, Film Maker

1. To stop spending my money on useless things and keep some for a change.

2. To stop being lazy and getting up late all the time.

3. To write and direct two movies starring Jennifer Aniston and to do the sex scenes myself.

History of Art Student

1. To try and grow and build a life, without being materially driven.

2. Lack of self-confidence. Laziness.

3. Personally: to learn as much as I possibly can, to be true to myself and honest with others. Globally: peace, consideration for everyone, everywhere.

Lecturer of Art

1. To work hard, bring up my children to want to learn, to respect the world and everyone in it. To finally find time to launch an exhibition of my work. A two week break to a Euro city every year of the millennium that I'm alive with my partner.

2. Bad organisation of my life, procrastination, lack of desire/time to fulfil my creative potential as an artist.

3. On 31 December get together all of our friends at our house with plenty of wine, good cheer, good food, love and hope. Globally, disappearance of heroin off the face of the earth, rebirth of Irish language, more thatched cottages!

Chapter 15

FARMERS, TRADERS AND TRAVELLERS

FARMERS

James O'Neill

1. To promote a cleaner environment and more awareness of our environment.

2. I would prefer to be positive and say I will endeavour to enhance my farm and surroundings.

3. Personally: I would like more understanding from urban dwellers about rural and farming ways of life. Peace all over the world.

John Nolan

1. Give up farming.

2. I don't know, I need them all.

3. Feed the world – up cattle, sheep and dairy prices.

Patrick J Walsh

1. That farming will improve or we're gone.

2. Working for nothing.

3. To retire and enjoy a few years of good health.

P M

1. Farming weather to do a U-turn. Ray Burke to become leader of Fianna Fáil.

2. Working harder for a living.

3. To find an easier way of life. To win £500,000 in the Lotto.

Farmer

1. To be a better person.

2. Drinking.

3. Good health, peace and wealth for all!

Moore Street Traders

Mary

1. Giving more to others.

2. Being nasty to others.

3. Keep my children on the right road. Give more money to Turkey.

Mary

1. To try and win Lotto and give some to Temple Street Children's Hospital.

2. Smoking.

3. Give more money to poor. Peace in world.

Mary

1. None.

2. Nothing.

3. Carry on as I am. Peace.

Mary

1. Pray for peace in Ireland.

2. Nothing to give up.

3. Peace in my home. Good to do something for children.

Pauline

1. Give up smoking, lose loads of weight, wear a mini and get plenty of bonking.

2. My husband.

3. To win the Lotto, peace in my house.

Teresa

1. Give up working.

2. Drunk.

3. Get divorced, have a divorce party. Moore Street staying the way it is and keep enjoying the craic.

Thomas

1. Better myself.

2. Try and give up drinking.

3. Own my own house and business, stop racism.

Vera

1. Don't have one.

2. Work.

3. Good health, justice.

TRAVELLERS

Ann

1. Let it go as it comes.

2. Leave worries behind.

3. I've only bad dreams. Hope for children. Hope to see everyone well.

Geraldine

1. I wouldn't know what to make.

2. Fags.

3. Own my own house some day. Everyone in the equal.

Luke

1. Haven't a clue.

2. Drink.

3. To have a lovely new house. For everyone to be better off.

Mary, Age 10

1. Better at school. Better at doing work for mum.

2. Giving out to mum.

3. To get bigger. I have loads of dreams. Win the Lotto. Give people in need half the money. I would like to clean up for my granny.

Nan, Age 6

1. To get better at school.

2. Tea.

3. That I could stay with my granny. Everyone in need to have money.

William

1. Hoping to get a younger woman.

2. Drunk.

3. Drive a Rolls Royce with a younger woman. Everyone to be rich.

William, Age 16

1. Be better at school.

2. Smoking.

3. Own a car, hope to get rich. Poor to get jobs.

Chapter 16

MEDICS MATTER

Magdalene Bristow,
Nurse and Lecturer in Women's Health

1. To continue my work with women's groups, encouraging them to take more control of their lives.

2. Living my life in a perpetual state of chaos.

3. A cure for cancer. Continued good health, happiness for my children and grandchildren.

Denis Curtin, Dentist

1. To continue to live one day at a time.

2. Overreacting to situations.

3. To see my son mature and be independent, and I hope that materialism will be brought under control.

Clare Gormley, Dental Nurse

1. To, as usual, try to be nice to all people I meet.

2. Stop smoking (as it is every year).

3. To really make recycling a habit in life.

Frances Heeny, Psychotherapist

1. To look towards wholeness in all areas of my life.

2. Procrastination. Negative thinking.

3. Personally: to pursue my career as a psychotherapist and consultant. Globally: peace in fullness for all.

Barbara Lynch, Nurse/Psychotherapist

1. To go to the theatre and the movies once a month. To save one pound per day.

2. To be less straight and less tired, which equals more fun.

3. Personally: to be able to make a complete professional change. Globally: peace in Northern Ireland. Bill Clinton to stay President.

Breda Murray, Retired Pharmacist

1. To lose one and a half stone in weight. Make new friends, broaden my horizons. Do some mural studies in Trinity. Improve my German. Travel more.

2. Overeating. Thinking I can solve everyone else's problems.

3. Personally: to get involved and work with some caring organisation. Globally: to see world peace and poverty abolished.

Marie White, Nurse

1. More hill walking.

2. Eating too much.

3. To drive through Paris in an open-topped car.

Christine, Registered Nurse

1. To investigate the possibility of a career change, in the private sector. Look at courses available in colleges. A possible change of property.

2. I would like to give up sugar and lose some weight, maybe join a sports club.

3. I would like to be happy, healthy and have more quality time to myself. To see Scotland gaining more power and independence within Europe and bring in the New Year at home. Hoping the year 2000 brings me lots of good luck – to travel more.

Eileen, Medical Secretary

1. To get fit enough to trek in the Eastern Himalayas and explore Bhutan's elusive kingdom.

2. Leaving getting fit until the 11th hour.

3. Personally: to meet and mingle with as many people of other cultures as possible. Globally: to see further breakdowns in racism and intolerance.

John, Medical Researcher

1. My resolution is to develop the habits of thinking more positively, acting more assertively and feeling more confident each day – starting before the millennium. I resolve also to shave more often, and not just when my girlfriend nags me to. I will try very hard to think nicer thoughts about my frightful neighbours, though I hope to be spared spending the next thousand years with them.

2. I would gladly abandon the following traits: my insomnia, skipping meals, my mild addiction to potato crisps, my inability to cook. I would like to dilute my intensity, seriousness and obsessiveness. My tendency to spend too much time alone. My habit of singing German war songs in the bath before learning the words properly.

3. Personally, I aspire to a radical shift in lifestyle. Paramount is a career change, to become self-employed in a more commercial direction. I would also like to marry, and move to a quiet house in the countryside. In the longer term, I might like to dip my toe in the water of politics. Globally, I would like to see a revival of Christianity in order to secure the future of Western 'civilisation'. I would welcome in particular a renewed emphasis on the centrality of good and evil, and the importance of family values in underpinning society. The Jews have a great deal to teach us in these respects, and the millennium is the right time to return to our common heritage. Would there be any chance that the Irish government could hire Margaret Thatcher to sort out our trade unions once and for all, as she did in Britain?

Dr M K, Psychiatrist

1. Stop making resolutions.

2. Perfection.

3. I never remember my dreams.

Medical Doctor

1. Lose weight – become healthier. Learn French. Work less.

2. Over-drinking. Being disorganised and procrastinating.

3. Get involved with some charity directly. Globally: See my children succeed – be more supportive. Write a book!

Psychologist

1. Just to be happy with people.

2. I would like to give up some of my conflicts that I find difficult to cope with.

3. Personally: I will be at one with my age and be able to spend my life with people. Globally: stop war everywhere, stop people from dying of the aftermath of poverty, injustice, abuse, violence, drugs. Adults pay more attention to childhood, family, older people, environment.

Chapter 17

THOSE WITH THE
MIDAS TOUCH

Tanya Airey, Managing Director,
Sunway Travel Group

1. Work smarter – not harder.

2. The bad ones.

3. Personally: to make sure my kids know what I look like and stay married. Globally: a world where no one goes hungry.

Louis Copeland, Tailor and Retailer of the
Year (Menswear) Ireland and UK, 1998-1999

1. Try and dress myself up for the millennium.

2. Not dressing myself up.

3. Good health for family. Peace in world.

Marguerite Dodds, Company Director, New Century Media Ltd

1. To achieve a good balance between work and leisure.

2. Worrying.

3. Personally: to become a good tennis player from a very late start. Globally: to banish war in the name of 'religion'.

Paul Duggan, Director, Unidare PLC

1. None, I don't believe in resolutions based on the arbitrary rotation of the earth around the sun.

2. None.

3. None in particular.

John Hamill, Engineer and Director, Comsat Associates, Ltd

1. To take each day as it comes and change only the things that I can change.

2. To be less judgmental and worrying.

3. To continue my own inner journey to peace and in doing so play a part in achieving world peace.

Rick Hetherington,
Managing Director and CEO, TV3

1. To help rid the world of government subsidised businesses!

2. My impatience with those who are constantly late.

3. To get my life in such order that I could live part of each year in Europe and North America. Globally, give everyone the chance to learn to read and write. Empowerment is the only way we can overcome our challenges.

Mary Hickey,
Housewife/Mother/Company Director

1. I want to get more organised. I run a small business (from home) and find that I am so busy that I have no time for myself. I want to take time for relaxation and interests.

2. I wish I didn't take life so seriously. I would like to be more witty and interesting.

3. I would like to see a just peace in troubled parts of the world. Support to be available for anyone finding it hard to cope. Personally, more free time and catch up with friends, etc.

Edwin Higel, Publisher and
Managing Director, New Island Books

1. Is this for one year or 1,000 years? I would like to have my next millennium more organised than the last one.

2. Sense of direction.

3. To live and work with friends. Less conflict.

Michael McDonnell,
Group Chief Executive, CIE

1. To continue with all my colleagues in the CIE Group to improve the quality of Irish public transport to bring it up to the best international standards.

2. Smoking.

3. Peace in Ireland and throughout the world.

Mike McDonnell, Director,
Institute of Personal Development (Ireland)

1. To refocus my priorities and try to get a better balance between work and other activities.

2. To be less afflicted by 'analysis paralysis' and become more of a risk taker.

3. To achieve a state of inner peace, and to see a world emerge where the value of diversity is recognised.

Arnold O'Byrne, Managing Director,
Opel Ireland

1. Not to make resolutions. You get guilt complexes and realise how weak-willed you are.

2. Leave a certain stubbornness behind.

3. Personally: continue to be happy. I'm married to the same person for 41 years. I thank God for this – to have found a good partner. Globally: for us all to accept and understand each other. Fear often makes us reject others.

Rory O'Connor, Manager

1. Lose weight!

2. Lack of exercise.

3. New marina for Rosses Point. New manager and team for Sligo Rovers. Successful Model Arts Centre in Sligo.

Chapter 18

TOTS TO TEENS

Alex Clarke, Age 6

1. Love someone more.

2. Try not to be grounded.

3. To have a baby animal farm, playing and to be happy.

Bruce Devine, Age 6¾

1. Making something out of boxes. Making space ships.

2. Giving up my Rubiks cube.

3. Personally: that I'll get into a real space suit. That I could go into a rocket ship. That I could go into a rocket ship with my suit on. That I could blast off. Globally: to make life a fair place for everyone. To see everyone's garden looking nice so everyone could play soccer and not fall in the mud. All the animals having fun.

Patrick Doyle, Age 8

1. Getting a new computer.

2. Chocolate things.

3. Everyone gets a free car for the year 2000.

Gary McLean, Age 11

1. A new bike.

2. I would give up Mars bars.

3. School at home.

Tracey O'Connor, Age 10

1. Take the goat for a walk.

2. Computer games and staying inside all day.

3. That all my daydreams will come true.

Nicky Roberts, Age 9

1. Not to say bad words.

2. Sweets.

3. A new dog.

Dervla, Age 8

1. Play soccer.

2. Give up going to ballet.

3. Dreams: to won a horse. To end war in Kosovo. Car.

Sarah, Age 5

1. To hoover, put down carpet, do washing up.

2. Leaving bedroom in a mess.

3. All my dreams are about cats and dogs. I would like everyone to have a cat.

FIRST YEAR STUDENTS AT
SECONDARY SCHOOL

Mark Cole

1. To stop telling lies.

2. To stop being rude and bold.

3. My dreams are that Northern Ireland and Ireland will be united.

Niamh Dolan

1. To stop eating a lot of crisps and do better in my school year this term.

2. I have to give up messing with my rings on my fingers when I get nervous.

3. To do well in all my exams (and meet Boyzone!).

Marie Hynes

1. To try better in school.

2. Stop biting my nails and lying.

3. Mine personally would be to become a teacher. Mine globally would be for peace in Northern Ireland.

Philip Kelly

1. To make no more resolutions.

2. Putting words in other people's mouths.

3. Personally: I like to have a computer career and Internet access. Globally: peace in the North.

Carolyn McKeon

1. To stop drinking fizzy drinks.

2. To stop growing my nails too long.

3. There will be world peace and everybody will have basic rights. For no more starving people in the world.

Brenda-Lisa McLoughlin

1. To stop chewing the tops of my pens.

2. To stop growing my nails so long.

3. For peace on earth.

James Molloy

1. To help at home.

2. To stop hurting my brother.

3. To become a truck driver.

Ben Mulligan

1. To train harder for soccer.

2. Playing computer too much.

3. For Manchester to buy some good football players.

Edel O'Sullivan

1. Be less sarcastic.

2. Don't fight!

3. All wars end and have world peace.

Eóin Phelan

1. My resolution for the millennium would be to do well in school.

2. I don't have a personal trait.

3. My dreams for the millennium would be that there will be no more war.

Christopher Tobin

1. To stop getting in trouble.

2. Blank.

3. World peace and a free occupied Ireland.

Student

1. To be nicer to my friends and family.

2. Being smart.

3. To be better at b-ball.

Student

1. Do well in school.

2. Give up smoking.

3. To do good in my exams and get a good job.

Student

1. To do well in school and go out with Fintan.

2. Swearing and smoking.

3. World peace and be famous.

Student

1. To work harder in school.

2. To stop spitting.

3. I hope the first-year basketball team will win the league.

Student

1. To be nice to people and to work hard in school.

2. To stop biting my nails so much.

3. To stop all the wars.

Student

1. Stop biting my nails.

2. Stop fighting with my sister.

3. To go out with Brian Forster! To meet Manchester United.

Student

1. In the millennium I would like to put a bit more weight on.

2. To be honest I'm happy the way I am but want to eat healthier foods.

3. I would like to be a premier league and play for Arsenal.

TRANSITION YEAR STUDENTS

Eimear Burke

1. Have a healthier lifestyle, get a job.

2. Lying.

3. Peace and a cleaner environment.

Tracy Cahill

1. Be nice.

2. Eating every hour of the day.

3. World peace.

Nollaig Lyons

1. To travel abroad.

2. Horrible personalities.

3. Make money, get a job. Sydney 2000.

Aoife McNulty

1. Study, decide on a career.

2. Shyness.

3. World peace, good food.

Aisling O'Connor

1. To travel the world in 80 days, just like Phineas Fogg.

2. Sarcasm, meanness, laziness.

3. World peace, end to hunger. Personal, to study twice as hard as before for my leaving certificate.

Ciara O'Connor

1. To study more.

2. My quick temper.

3. To stop global warming.

Audrey Persse

1. To study hard.

2. Messy handwriting.

3. To get on well with everyone.

Student

1. To meet Jason McAteer once and for all. To work hard for my leaving cert. To help the Third World work for a better environment. To shop 'til I drop.

2. I would like to give up spending and my disorganisation.

3. World peace, cleaner environment, no hunger, no landmines and Bill Clinton to have stepped down.

Sixth Year Students in Secondary School

Pat Heffernen

1. To give up smoking, do what I want to do and enjoy myself doing it.

2. I would like to be able to stop smoking and drink less.

3. I would like to cover the country in oak tress like it's supposed to be and watch them grow into the new millennium.

Trish Kearns

1. To be content in myself and be grateful for what I have. To be happy.

2. I'd like to be less possessive, more giving and less bitchy.

3. I would like to be a better person, to be good at my job and to see a cutback in pollution and nuclear weapon development in the world.

Niall Kelly

1. I will try harder at succeeding in any work I do.

2. I would like to be a better person.

3. I would like to travel and see the world for a year or two.

Joyce Maloney

1. To travel and meet more people. Do a lot more and be the best I can.

2. To give up shouting so much. To be a nicer person.

3. To travel to America and work in the summer camps.

Johanna Murray

1. That whatever I do, I do it with the utmost style and conviction.

2. Stop bitchiness. Stop defensiveness. Stop living in the sadness and mistakes of the past.

3. Personally: to do well in my leaving cert and find something that is really worthwhile to do. Globally: to see less economic divisions in society. Have opportunities available for all.

Ruth O'Brien

1. Stay exactly the way I am now or will be then.

2. None, because they make me different. Everyone has to be a little annoying.

3. Becoming an actress or nurse and hopefully avoiding Judgment Day.

Garvan O'Keeffe

1. I'd like to become more open-minded about other people's problems.

2. My selfishness.

3. I wouldn't mind if people just learned to get along and accept everybody for what they are.

Eoghan Parle

1. Give up smoking.

2. Better application to do things.

3. United Ireland.

Chapter 19

DOWN THROUGH THE AGES

Twenty Somethings

Leah Baker, UCD Student

1. To pursue a career I'm really interested in that will be challenging and rewarding. Before I do this, however, I would like to travel to South America.

2. Insecurity with my self-image. Inability to make the right decisions at moments when, presented with the opportunity, I consciously make the wrong one and feel remorseful afterwards, especially for the fact that I know I'm making the wrong decision at the time.

3. I hope the millennium will bring a wider perspective of the world through travel. I would like to in some way be an ambassador for my country. Globally, I'm not sure; I have enough insecurities and uncertainties about my own future to think on such a level. But obviously, and I suppose somewhat superficially, I'd like for all countries affected by war and natural disasters to be aided in every possible way in building a future for their country. The work of Christina Noble and her Sunshine Foundation for the street

children in Vietnam particularly moved me and made me take an interest in helping others, which would be rewarding on a personal level, whilst also helping out on a global level.

William Dowling, UCD Student

1. To improve my musical skills.

2. Impatience.

3. Personally: to get married. To be successful in whatever my career path is. Globally: world peace.

Mary Clare Flynn

1. Personal fulfilment.

2. Worry/anxiety. Smoking. Saying yes when I want to say no.

3. Personally: to be happy and fulfilled. Globally: people would be more aware of their spirituality.

Jenna Hammer, Student

1. Graduate college and hopefully get a real job.

2. Occasionally interrupting people.

3. I hope the majority of people remain calm and don't go crazy (in a bad way) on December 31st 1999.

Emma Hennigan, UCD Student

1. To be a better person.

2. Being dependent on others, being impatient.

3. Personally: to see the world, further my education and expand my understanding of other people. Globally: resolve environmental and political problems.

Tara Hickey, Research Psychology Student

1. I have made no resolutions. I never make them because I can never be bothered to make them. I'm not interested in them.

2. I can be stubborn, I would like to be more organised.

3. To get on the clinical psychology course, buy an apartment, invest money and become business-

wise, travel to several countries. Live in various countries. Gain new experience, personally and in my occupation. Be successful both in work and my relationship.

Sinead Hughes

1. To live each day to the full.

2. I would like to give up time-wasting and moaning about situations which I am too bloody lazy to alter.

3. I would like to create a more harmonious environment for myself and others.

Aislinn O'Brien, UCD Student

1. Stop smoking.

2. Laziness.

3. Travel, make money, have sex.

N O'Murchu, Engineer

1. Get laid. Learn to drive.

2. Smoking. Laziness.

3. Personally: fall in love. Globally: be more environmentally conscious.

Jen Reiger, Student

1. To live each day to the fullest, because life is precious.

2. Nail-biting, Cadbury-eating, close-mindedness.

3. For the world to remain ethnically diverse within the presence of the current global community.

Catherine, Student

1. To write a book. To give up smoking. To have more sex.

2. To be less of a perfectionist and to be more assertive.

3. I'd like to be married by the millennium and have a good job with lots of money.

Woman, Student of Psychology

1. To stop thinking too much about irrelevant things and begin to relax and enjoy life more.

2. Laziness (mental and physical laziness). Lack of motivation to work hard.

3. To go to space with my family. To abolish hard college exams.

THIRTY SOMETHINGS

Louise McKennedy,
Teacher/Wife/Mother/Cook/Tidy-upper

1. To be nine and a half stone again. Not to give out. To get fit.

2. Impatience. Tidy up my clothes in the bedroom. Don't give out when John is driving.

3. To be a good mother, wife, teacher and friend. Peace.

Colette Mullaney, Chef

1. Risk more!! Love myself.

2. Negative thoughts. Fear of failure.

3. Peace. Joy. Acceptance of others and ourselves.

Rory O'Connor, "Student of the World"

1. To continue to deny the validity of the millennium and to work tirelessly for the dissolution of the Christian conspiracy with the bearded man.

2. Sanity.

3. See 1 and 2 above.

Mary Ryan, Cleaner

1. To become pregnant and hopefully have twins.

2. To stop trying to prevent little lines on my face.

3. To be a wonderful human being.

Guidance Counsellor

1. To travel.

2. None.

3. World peace and my own business.

Anonymous Man

1. To be more decisive and more tolerant in my work relationships.

2. Being too aggressive and drinking too much alcohol as a way of coping with difficult situations.

3. Personally: peace and happiness. Globally: an end to world poverty, a redistribution of wealth and a lasting peace to settle over the world. More international understanding. More tolerance of different cultures and ways of life. Less narrow-minded bigotry. Less selfishness and one-up manship.

Anonymous Woman

1. To prioritise more effectively. Better balance between work and private life.

2. Being in control – learn to delegate and relax. Don't get things out of proportion.

3. Personally: to be happy, enjoy life and have no regrets. Globally: more co-operation internationally and less paranoia.

FORTY SOMETHINGS

John M Kennedy, Deputy Principal

1. To keep fit.

2. Being late.

3. To be the number one vintage squash player in Ireland. World literacy.

Elizabeth Lawlor

1. To slow down the pace of life.

2. Unwillingness to participate in physical exercise.

3. To take life at a more leisurely pace.

Judy McLoughlin, Student Counsellor

1. To live in the "now".

2. Anxiety, selfishness.

3. Peace of mind in knowing who I am and fulfilling my potentials. Globally, I pray for peace and justice for all.

Audrey Pritchard, Housewife

1. To take up a completely new interest – live life to its full and take steps to stay fit and healthy!

2. Self-doubt, worrying about the things I cannot change.

3. Personally: to have the time and money to travel around the world first class! Globally: a cure for cancer, an equitable distribution of food and wealth. To slow down, and (of course) peace.

Niall P Pritchard, Loss Adjustor

1. To be more self-determined.

2. Putting things on the long finger.

3. Self-contentment and peace.

Hilda

1. Never look back.

2. Being in bed by 10.00 pm every night.

3. To spend more time daydreaming, the most recognised form of relaxation. To see shops and service open 24 hours. A pill instead of sleep for 24 hour living.

Maggie

1. Be more tolerant of others and myself. Try to change what can be changed for the better. Enjoy life and see the humorous side.

2. Couch potato syndrome.

3. Naturally for peace, no starvation, good families. For people to have a dream come true and not worry about what they have missed along the way. That I can be at peace with my choices and as the saying goes, "have serenity to accept the things I cannot change, the courage to change the things I can and the wisdom to know the difference".

Maria

1. Good health.

2. Lack of confidence.

3. Personally: contentment and job satisfaction. Globally: better support for cancer patients.

Anonymous Man

1. To be more self-determined.

2. Putting things on the long finger.

3. Self-contentment and peace.

FIFTY SOMETHINGS

Kieran Conway, Businessman

1. To lose three stone weight.

2. Overeating.

3. I would like to see the end of famine in the world and I would like to see Third World debt written off by the World Bank.

Patricia Kennedy

1. To be a woman with attitude and push out the boundaries.

2. To be less cynical.

3. Improve my mind and spoil myself discreetly.

Mary O'Brien

1. To live each day fully.

3. To enjoy more time with my husband and my adult "children" and my future grandchildren. To have peace in our own country and worldwide.

Gerry O'Rourke, Technician

1. To quit cigarettes.

2. To stop being a couch potato and television addict.

3. To get fit.

Nora O'Sullivan, Retired Civil Servant

1. To travel more and renew old friendships.

2. Overeating and to become more fit.

3. A united Ireland before halfway through the new century. To have a greater sense of awareness for the needs of the less privileged in society.

Mona Walshe

1. To be conscious of time and to use it well.

2. Eating too much.

3. That peace may continue in Ireland and throughout the world and that Ireland may continue to prosper.

Margaret

1. More acceptance of foibles of family members.

2. To let chocolates and buns take a back seat in my life.

3. To be different is not to be perceived as a weakness. That children are listened to and do not dominate.

Sean

1. To learn to give.

2. Not having to work so much.

3. Buy lots of property. Peace. More money for children's hospitals.

Anonymous Man

1. I rather doubt there will be one; personal resolutions rather tend to fall by the wayside.

2. I'm not sure that there are any traits sufficiently awful that they need to be given up – though I would concede that my family might disagree.

3. Personally: to attain a reasonable degree – then think again. Globally: that the large number of dictators, despots and other nasties in power throughout the world be greatly reduced.

Anonymous Woman,
Devoted Mother and Housewife

1. Travel, learn to drive.

2. Worrying too much about others – let them go to hell (sometimes)!

3. Less alcohol (the silent drug). For people to take more interest in nature. I would like to see people becoming more tolerant.

SIXTY SOMETHINGS

Deirdre Daly

1. To live well into the new millennium.

2. Sometimes making impulsive decisions.

3. More global peace.

Kathleen Moran

1. To stand up for truth, no matter what the cost.

2. Thinking about what people think of me. Letting it bother me.

3. Personally: to try to be more selfless. Globally: the cancellation of the world debt in poor countries.

Pat Murray

1. To be myself. Only myself. Fully myself and nothing but myself. (Self = meaning the "Self" created by the Creator. Distinguish between peripheral and essential.)

2. Selfishness.

3. Answered in number one.

Joseph O'Loin

1. I would like to see my children and grandchildren financially settled.

2. I would like to curtail my drinking.

3. Peace in the world and end to violence in Northern Ireland.

Jerry O'Sullivan, Builder

1. To maintain fitness and health so as to be able to avail of all of the opportunities to travel around the world.

2. Alcohol, less smoking of the pipe and the patience to suffer fools gladly.

3. A peaceful and united Ireland. That the European Union would continue to grow and benefit us all. That the Fianna Fáil party will survive their difficulties and lead us into the millennium.

SEVENTY SOMETHINGS

Sister M Aquin Enright, Missionary Sister

1. To be more Christ-like in thoughts, words and deeds.

2. A critical attitude.

3. Personally: to be more Christ-centered and prayer-filled. Globally: the return of Christian values in homes and workplaces, countries and governments.

Sister Marie Tehan, Teacher/Nurse/Social Work/Psychologist/Home Economist

1. To live every day to the full.

2. Selfishness, an ingrained tendency to be a very private person.

3. Personally: that I do my best for everyone whose lives I touch. Globally: that we care for each other and forget the "rat race" for money after living and working for 50 years in Nigeria and Ethiopia.

EIGHTY SOMETHINGS

Sister Mark Cahir, Missionary Sister

1. My resolution for the millennium will be to aim at seeing Christ in every circumstance of my life and in each person with whom I come in contact. In order to help me towards this I hope to give more time to scripture and personal prayer.

2. Being judgmental and critical of my neighbours.

3. That I may grow closer to Christ and in the service of my neighbour. Globally: I would hope for a more even distribution of God's gifts, for peace and justice and that all people may come to the knowledge of Christ and has Christ.

Sister M Bede Kearns O P, Retired Teacher

1. To make the new century one of peace, goodwill, and true values in life, especially in the lives of young people. I begin with my own life, doing my best for real justice, respect for others, practising what I preach.

2. At this stage of my life, I need a stick when out walking. I am inclined to ponder on the well-meant kindness of the many people who offer to escort me across the road, carry parcels, etc. I cannot believe I am in my 80s.

3. To see real peace and understanding amongst individuals, nations, different religions. My life-long contact with young people has shown me the goodness latent in all. I would love to see that grow and spread in the world.

Sister Maria Malone

1. To try to live from my own inner core.

2. Impetuousity, arrogance, judgmental attitudes, gossip, etc.

3. A renewal of Christianity – personally, nationally and globally.

Michael McMahon

1. To be more kind and tolerant to everyone that I meet.

2. To be less meticulous.

3. To be spared to enjoy the millennium and hope for a less violent world.

Maura Roche, Pub Owner

1. Make the most of my time and become a better artist.

2. Forgetfulness, carelessness.

3. Personally: a good life for my children, grand-children and great-grandchildren. Globally: a utopia – peace, justice and no more capitalistic society.

Sister Mary Walsh

1. My resolution for the millennium will be to con-tinue to pray to our God of Love, who destined His children to arrive at the fullness of the Christ-ian life. That such may be a reality in this life and that I may not see death until I become what He wants me to be.

2. Very many – selflessness, lack of generosity, jeal-ousy, letting go of hurts in the past, resentment, distraction in prayer.

3. That peace and justice may reign in our world, that it may be a better place to live in, especially for the poor, the lonely, the unloved. That youth will resist drugs, obey God's laws, say "no" to abortion, divorce and un-Christian living, that homes may be happy places for all to live in. That ecumenism may become a reality and that all may be one in truth.

NINETY SOMETHINGS

May Anderson

1. A better life.

2. Worrying about the future.

3. Peace for the whole world. A nice home life. To be in my own home again. I would like to meet my husband and relations again.

Kathleen Boothman, Housewife

1. School children trained to leave school at 16 and get proper training for work.

2. Being involved with carelessness in everyday life – especially cigarette ash left on schools!

3. Less subject ads on television conveying living at its worst. How can our children understand?

Mary Coyle, Housewife

1. To try to understand other people better.

2. My habit of having a low opinion and dislike of some people.

3. Tranquillity for myself and peace. Globally, an improvement in human rights.

Mary Dermady

1. Health and exercise.

2. Nothing to change.

3. Remain independent and keep up with national news. Peace.

Joshua Dowling

1. To remain alive.

2. Unnecessary worry (daily chores).

3. To continue to have good health and good relationships with family. Peace in the world.

Sister M Columba McGeady, Retired Teacher

1. To use opportunities to deepen my prayer life.

2. The inability to attend to immediate things, i.e. letters needing replies, etc.

3. Personally: to see peace firmly established in Northern Ireland. Globally: for justice and peace throughout the world. That our government would be conscious of the homeless in our midst and care for them.

Anonymous Woman, Retired Missioner

1. As an 89½ year old missionary sister, my resolution is to look forward to death.

2. Any egotistical traits.

3. John the Baptist's words: "He must increase – I must decrease."

ONE HUNDRED SOMETHINGS

Bill King

1. To live what time I have left and to "be in touch" as long as I can.

2. Be happy and grateful for what has been. No regrets or hindsights – just catch up with what's going on now!

3. Personally: good health out to the end. Globally: peace and justice throughout the world.

Bea O'Leary

1. To be happier.

2. Cold, wet days.

3. A lot of things – to have money enough to eat well and be contented. That thought never entered my head. We always thought of ourselves.

Chapter 20

ALL KINDS OF EVERYTHING

Francis Barrett, Labourer and Boxer

1. To qualify for the Olympics and win a medal.

2. Cannot think of any but would like to show more patience when shopping with the wife.

3. Personally: reach the Olympics, win a medal. Globally: less hate in the world and more love, peace and understanding between all.

Dorothy Barry, Chief Executive, Míle átha Cliath, Dublin's Millennium Partnership

1. To carry less baggage, physical and psychological. I can only read one book at a time.

2. Eating crisps.

3. A better, kinder world. A rebuilding of communities. Peace in our country.

Brian Boylan, Hotel Manager

1. Concern for the poor (and planet, etc.).

2. Materialism.

3. Spend as much on the poor as on the Millennium Dome, etc.

Veronica Byrne, Administrator, Swim Ireland

1. To travel to Sydney and watch a full Irish swimming team participate.

2. Stress.

3. Global peace, increase in number of endangered animals. 50m pool in Ireland.

Teresa Cashman, Housewife and Mother

1. To rear my family.

2. Lack of confidence and assertiveness.

3. Personally: to be healthy, successful. Globally: education for all.

John Fallon, Plumber

1. To be a good father and good provider.

2. Give up smoking.

3. Get a house and eventually live outside Dublin. NATO out of Kosovo. British out of Ireland. Peace in world.

Brian Graham, Trainee Counsellor

1. To continue to study and qualify further after my diploma.

2. Being negative and lack of confidence.

3. To qualify as a counsellor and be working with people with alcohol/drug problems.

Niall Grant, Firefighter

1. One has one shot at life on this earth – treat it like a holiday – to make the most of what life has to offer me (good/bad) – hopefully learn another language!

2. Stop putting people into categories, i.e. generalising about the person's statue in life or their colour, etc.

3. Personally: financially secure in my mid-life, healthy and happily married. Only two of which I have control over. Globally: that people involved with world politics stop acting like spoiled children and begin to take control of real world issues. World peace is a lovely thought but will never happen until countries learn to cope with their own internal problems first. So for the next millennium, the biggest dream I have is not a global one but that the troubles between the two religions in this country come to an end. I pray to see it in my lifetime. Life is too short for such small-mindedness.

Francis Hester, Garda Síochána

1. My resolution for the millennium is for personal happiness and enjoyment in life, and to be kind in my dealings with others.

2. I am happy with my lifestyle and I have no wish to give up any of my personal traits.

3. Personally: to have the opportunity to pursue personal goals. Globally: peaceful world and greater equality in the world.

Aideen Laurent, National School Teacher

1. To decorate the house. To start painting again (personal).

2. Putting things on the long finger.

3. End of abuse, environmental damage. That people start to consider the feelings of others. People have stopped caring/respecting others.

Breda O'Rourke, Retired Civil Servant

1. Keep weight down. Be more positive.

2. To be tolerant of others.

3. Better health. World peace.

Mary Manton

1. To live my life in a way that will help others to understand those of us with a disability.

2. Frustration.

3. Live my life in a way that is no different than anyone else's. A better world – not too materialistic.

P Medley, Private Tenant's Advisor

1. To get closer to my maker.

2. Anxiousness.

3. World peace.

Ann Murphy, Office Worker

1. Allocate more time to my health-consciousness. More exercise, use of alternative health remedies and contribute to a cleaner, healthier environment.

2. Rather than keep criticising governments or communities/organisations, have more active contribution to these bodies.

3. A healthier, peaceful and more accepting environment for me, locally and globally. Less wars, famines, and more justice and peace for all, but in particular in our non-democratic establishments.

John Phillips, Financial Analyst

3. An independent Scotland with a more economically unified Europe.

C M Ryan, Chef

1. To be more positive in the way I think. Also, to understand people better.

2. Smoking.

3. Dreams: become rich and successful. Personally: I would like to travel to interesting countries and to have a successful relationship. Aspirations: to live life to its full.

Christina Smyth, Housewife and Businesswoman

1. Travel. Help others.

2. Not to worry about my weight. To accept myself and be happy.

3. World peace, child abuse to end and love to always remain.

Liam Walshe, Retired Garda Chief Superintendent

1. To remain healthy, to enjoy life. To travel as much as possible, and have good holidays. To enjoy good food and drink, but to partake of it moderately.

2. To be free, and not to be restrained in any way by my past, tradition, culture, or any other fears that may have a restraining effect. To be in flow.

3. Peace, prosperity on this island. Justice and peace worldwide. A good healthy attitude to life – to be happy and also my family unit to be happy and content.

Josephine Ward, Retired Teacher

1. To spread peace as best I can. For example, to think peaceful thoughts, to make a gesture of peace to others when the opportunity comes, to pray that God will come into people's lives: "Christ be in all hearts thinking about me, Christ be in all tongues telling of me."

2. Judging and misjudging the actions of others.

3. An amnesty for all political prisoners all over the world. That the debt of third world countries be wiped out by the rich nations. That justice would prevail for us all – in Ireland because I live here, to remove tax on widows' pensions and lower income groups, etc. For God to become the centre of our lives.

Susan Ward, Solicitor

1. To give *myself* more time – the past fifteen years have been focused on family and the needs of the kids and David. Now that they are older I am going to be more in touch with what I want and need for myself.

2. Taking on too much at any one time. Overloading my personal timetable in an effort to please everyone and keep in touch with everyone.

3. If I survive 1999 one absolute certainty is that I will die in the millennium. My personal aspiration is therefore to face Death positively as a new beginning and my dream is that when it comes it proves to be something other than personal extinction but rather an exciting adventure.

   On a more specific note, I want to travel to every national park in North America; visit India, China, Russia, Burma, Australia and/or New Zealand, Antarctica, Hawaii (other places as yet undecided); I want to write a book that will be critically acclaimed by others (some chance!); I want to see all three of my children happy in their personal and working lives and self-sufficient; I want both my husband and myself to keep in good health and when we do drop down dead, I hope that it is immediate and final – when we are asleep and dreaming!

   In a global context my dream is for every individual to do to others as he/she would have them do to him/herself. Hopefully this would result in a general evaluation that peace is better than war and what occurs in other places or continents is of concern to each and every one of us. My other dream is that everyone looks to the substance of another individual rather than the external veneer/image and be prepared to hold others accountable for their actions rather than be indifferent to what is going on around them.

Retired Civil Servant

1. To give up spending money on National Lotto scratch cards.

2. Squandering my allowance fortnightly on lottery cards.

3. To win the Lotto on Saturday night.

Meditators, Ionad Folláin, Centre of Wholeness

Meditator

1. Be a good neighbour to all.

2. Self-indulgence.

3. Peace and tranquillity to all mankind.

Meditator

1. If I am still around I will listen more often to other people's points of view.

2. Not to think of myself but to do good deeds for others. Give up being selfish.

3. That people will rejoice and not give their elders and other people cause for alarm, but keep their celebrations peaceful.

Meditator

1. I won't make a resolution.

2. Learn to appreciate better what I have got.

3. A more just world – where caring for earth, all humans and all creatures replaces the present irrational greed and desire for possessions. A world where joy and laughter can be heard and replace the gloomy and empty expressions on so many faces. Personally, that I can contribute in my own little way to this.

Meditator

1. To treat everyone kindly and not hold grudges against any human being. To greet people kindly and wish everyone well.

2. Getting new clothes when I don't need them and to not lie in bed in the mornings.

3. That peace will reign in our hearts, in our families and in our country. That Man will really value the things of this earth given to us by our maker.

Meditator

1. To live joyfully and peacefully.

2. To allow love in and banish all fear.

3. Tolerance of differences and dialogue amongst Christians and other religions.

Meditator

1. To live in hope for a better Ireland.

2. Worrying about what other people think of me.

3. More information for the elderly to live in peace and without fear.

AN GAELTACHT

Micheál O'Domhnaill, Gaillimh Síuneir

1. Níl aon cheann pearsonta agam ach leanacht ar aghaidh san millaois nua mar a chriochnaigh mé an ceann seo caite.

2. Nach mbeadh airgead chomh tabhachtach dhom mar go bhfuil na rudaí is tabhachtaí sa saol seo anois agus amach romham saor in aisce. Freisin dha mbeach me anann chomhairle a thogáil ó dhuine eile.

3. Go mbeadh níos mó meas ar theanga na gaeltachta san tír so mar, níl aon cheo agat mar a bhfuil do theanga dhuchais féin agat. Go mbeadh níos mo áma agus airgead caithe ag torálocht leigheas ar ghalair agus tinneas. Ba mhaith liom a bheith mar athair mhaith agus a bheith mor athair go minic.

Mairtin O'H-Alin, Briceadoir

1. Ba mhaith liom teanga nua a folam agus dul ar aghaidh sa saol mar atá mé anois.

2. Ba mhaith liom gan a bheith leath chamh re-chuiseach agus atá mé, ach ní cheapainn go n-aroidh sé sin. Mar a deir an sean-fhochal "cur sioda ar ghabhar agus is ghabhan I gconaí e".

3. Ba mhaith daoine nua agus culturacha eile ar fud an domhain a fheiceal ague a cur in aithne. Ba mhaith liom deireadh a freiceal lé ciníochas mar is clann dé ar fad uirid.

PART III:

WRAPPING IT ALL UP

Chapter 21

PORTRAIT OF THE ARTISTS: IMPRESSIONS AND IMPRINTS

When I initially approached individuals to answer three questions I was in many ways requesting them to leave an imprint on a book that would be a legacy to the next generation. Many responded quickly and with enthusiasm. Others backed away, though, and said 'no way'. Some questioned the questions themselves. Others guessed at their answers while some ignored them and hoped I would not ask again. Of course, many replied but didn't want to have their name appear in lights.

In the beginning, when I distributed the questionnaires, I had no expectations. I felt that should I receive a few insightful or delightful thoughts from well-known politicians or entertainers, this might give the final product a spicy flavour. But as replies poured in, I became slightly greedy and decided to widen the pot. It then dawned on me that I needed to broaden my horizon and be more inclusive and allow children, teenagers and the elderly to express their views as well.

From the spontaneity of the young to the wisdom of the old, from the humour of the Moore Street traders to the warmth of the travellers, from the empathy of those helping others to the sense of fun from entertainers, a clearer picture emerged of the Irish people.

The answers were like pieces of a puzzle where

the final picture emerged when the last reply arrived. The impression that arises is a picture of a race steeped in fun, humour, wit, intelligence, empathy, confusion, honesty, hope, loyalty and a longing for both personal fulfilment and a beautiful country at peace with itself, as well as peace around the world.

However, each question's replies are indicative of where individuals are at in a certain stage of their lives. Children's answers show wonderful spontaneity, and they were not afraid to express their wishes. They also answered the questions quite literally, like Sarah, aged five, who said, "All my dreams are about cats and dogs."

Teenagers tend to concentrate on issues centred around school exams and desires to meet their heroes, like Jason McAteer, Boyzone, or their favourite soccer hero. They are in the process of getting to know themselves and becoming adults, and their answers clearly displayed this.

The twenty somethings show that they are starting to concentrate on careers, relationships and are environmentally conscious. At this stage, the world is their oyster while at the same time they are aware of their imperfections and are anxious to rectify these.

The thirty somethings are starting to prioritise and maintain their sense of fun and adventure yet are still prepared to take some risks. The 'forty somethings' want to slow down a bit and are more conscious of health, happiness and the ability to keep pursuing more options. Balance is strived for and tolerance is very much on the agenda.

Those in their fifties seem to have found new

energy as they mention their wish to travel to far-away places like Bhutan and are preparing to push out their boundaries. Whatever they failed to do earlier in life, they are trying to give it another go. The 'sixty somethings' are more aware of issues such as 'truth', 'self' and living well. They seem to have a sense of stillness and ease.

The seventy somethings also are conscious of living life to the full, while those in their eighties are aware of making the most of the time they have left. Finally, those who have reached ninety or even one hundred are still able to be independent and focus on the world around them.

Our politicians certainly emphasised their time-less mission to improve our country and their vision for a peaceful Ireland. Media people and entertainers showed their insight into how we all juggle roles that sometimes leave us exhausted, anxious and even negative. Those from the Church still strive for a better Christian world where God's love will embrace all humanity.

All our citizens – from composers to painters, from farmers to chief executives – display a general agreement that we all want a state of inner peace and that individuals want to have happiness and all their hopes, dreams and aspirations fulfilled, not forgotten. There is also an overwhelming desire for world peace and a commitment from all to respect human rights and the elimination of poverty, pain and persecution.

As we say goodbye to the 20th century and herald in a new era, I want to extend my sincere thanks to my very exclusive (yet inclusive) participants who willingly put pen to paper and helped create

Longings and Legacies. My aspiration is that all their dreams will come true and negativities will be left behind.

A huge and warm thank you goes out to each and every one of you and I wish you all a happy and peaceful new century.

Rubaiyat of Omar Khayyan of Naishapur

The Moving Finger writes; and, having writ,
Moves on: nor all your Piety nor Wit
Shall lure it back to cancel half a Line,
Nor all your Tears wash out a Word of it.

Translator: Edward Fitzgerald